A WORLD OUT OF BALANCE?

SPECIAL REPORT OF THE
CEPS MACROECONOMIC POLICY GROUP

DANIEL GROS, CEPS
THOMAS MAYER, DEUTSCHE BANK, LONDON
ANGEL UBIDE, TUDOR INVESTMENTS, WASHINGTON, D.C.

CENTRE FOR EUROPEAN POLICY STUDIES
BRUSSELS

This report presents the findings and recommendations of the CEPS Macroeconomic Policy Group (MPG), a select body of highly respected economists who have undertaken to carry out independent, in-depth research on current developments in the European economy. CEPS gratefully acknowledges financial support from Deutsche Bank, London and Tudor Investments for the work of the MPG. The views expressed in this report are those of the authors writing in a personal capacity and do not necessarily reflect those of CEPS or any other institution with which the members are associated.

ISBN 92-9079-621-9

Centre for European Policy Studies
Place du Congrès 1, B-1000 Brussels
Tel: 32 (0) 2 229.39.11 Fax: 32 (0) 2 219.41.51
e-mail: info@ceps.be
internet: http://www.ceps.be

CONTENTS

List of Tables

List of Figures

List of Boxes

Preface

This is the third special report issued by the CEPS Macroeconomic Policy Group since it was reconstituted in 1999, coinciding with the launch of monetary union in the EU. It is 'special' in the sense that it does not focus on current developments in the European economy, as do our usual annual reports, but rather on the imbalances that have developed in the global economy. 'Global imbalances' is the polite term adopted by policy-makers to describe the huge current account deficit of the US, but the term also captures an important aspect of this phenomenon: the fact that the US would not have been able to build up such an extraordinary deficit if other countries had not been willing to run very large surpluses. We capture this dynamic with the expression: 'It takes two to tango'.

What is the role of Europe in this global game? On the one hand, one could argue that Europe, and in particular the eurozone, is an innocent bystander as its external account remains more or less balanced. On the other hand, Europe has contributed to a widening of the US current account deficit and it has a vital interest in a resolution of these imbalances without too many frictions. The main theme of our report then is: how long can the present constellation of external imbalances last and will their resolution affect Europe?

We wish to acknowledge the valuable contribution of Selen Guerin, LUISS Research Fellow at CEPS. Funda Celikel provided excellent research assistance. All remaining errors are ours. Regular readers of the MPG reports will have noticed another feature that makes this report special, namely we have abandoned our traditional cover design of the green and purple-coloured blocks for an original drawing, for which we wish to thank our colleague Jorge Núñez Ferrer.

The work of the CEPS Macroeconomic Policy Group would not have been possible without the continuing support of our main sponsor, Deutsche Bank, London, and Tudor Investments of Washington, D.C. I wish to thank them once again for their material and financial contributions.

Daniel Gros
Director
April 2006

Non-Technical Summary

'It takes two to tango'. The unprecedented US current account deficit would not have been possible without the willingness of other countries to run equally unprecedented surpluses. So far, the two partners have moved in near-perfect synchronisation, with US households increasing consumption at the same pace that emerging markets and, more recently, oil exporters, were increasing savings. The dance has now reached such a frantic tempo, however, that it is not likely to go on much longer without the lead partner becoming exhausted. A gradual winding down is still possible, and indeed is likely, as demand growth in the US slows and the supply of savings from the rest of the world diminishes with investment in emerging markets increasing and consumption in oil-exporting countries also rising to reflect their greater wealth. Nevertheless, the longer the dance goes on, the more likely it becomes that an accident will occur because of a lack of synchronisation between the two main partners.

Serious problems for global financial markets could arise if one of the two dancers wants to continue and the other wants to quit.

For example, emerging markets and oil exporters might continue to remain large net savers, but the US might have used up its credit with financial markets because its debt is judged to have reached an unsustainable level. In that case, the dollar would decline sharply and US interest rates would have to increase even further. Other central banks, including the European Central Bank, might have to step in to prevent the global economy from sliding into recession. We regard this scenario as conceivable but unlikely for the time being.

But the opposite scenario also cannot be excluded: US policy-makers might want to continue to keep growth at its current pace, but emerging markets might no longer be willing to run large surpluses. In that case, financial markets would be buffeted by two opposing forces: faced with a slowing housing sector and an exhausted consumer, the Federal Reserve might start lowering short rates again to maintain the pace of expansion but, in order to keep the global savings-investment balance, global long-term real interest rates would have to increase sharply, bringing down asset prices until US consumption is brought in line with income. The willingness of the US authorities to accept a prolonged slowing of the US economy and thus avoid this scenario is likely to be tested soon.

Another risk is that the lead partner becomes overly confident and believes he can do a solo performance. That some US politicians are susceptible to this temptation is evidenced by calls for protection of US assets from foreign take-over, even restrictions on the purchase of US Treasuries by foreigners are being mooted. If this were really implemented, however, the music would stop and many of the dancers would lose their footing and some might even collapse to the floor.

Executive Summary

Over the last decade, the global economy has trod a dynamic path with ever-increasing US current account deficits financed by surpluses accumulated in emerging market economies. This report argues that this state of affairs has resulted from an exceptional and complex combination of events and policy responses that are unlikely to persist, requiring an adjustment soon in asset markets and the global economy.

We argue that the global supply of savings is likely to shrink soon, with investment in emerging markets growing strongly and consumption in oil-rich countries adjusting gradually to the windfall from high oil prices. This combination should lead to higher real interest rates and a cooling of real estate markets, with asymmetric effects on the US economy which should slow much more than the eurozone. A gradual resorption of the US external deficit is thus possible without a crash of the US dollar.

The key issue for this gradual adjustment is whether US policy-makers will accept a prolonged period of weaker growth: a *conditio sine qua non* for a reduction in the US external deficit towards more sustainable levels is a reduction of the growth rate in domestic demand by about 1 percentage point over several years. Since this lower US growth will likely drag down global growth, a cautious approach to the reduction of the US current account deficit is likely, with the adjustment taking place over a few business cycles. If, however, the process is unduly delayed by US policies resisting this necessary slowing down of domestic demand growth or by the rest of the world failing to pick up the baton, the odds of a disorderly adjustment will increase dramatically.

The US current account deficit has now reached 7% of GDP, beyond all previous historical records, but the perceived importance of this phenomenon seems to be declining. In fact, the policy discussion has become highly politicised, with a different consensus emerging in each of the affected geographical areas as to the cause of the current situation:

- the 'Washington consensus' blames China for under-consumption and a beggar-thy-neighbour exchange rate policy,

- the 'European consensus' blames the US fiscal deficit and the Fed's loose monetary policy and

- the 'Asian consensus' blames the US for over-consumption and sees the accumulation of foreign exchange reserves as an integral component of a managed floating exchange rate system.

One side effect of these conflicting views is a lack of any deep analysis of the problem, as most observers are motivated by a specific agenda.

This report tries to fill this gap by providing a comprehensive discussion of the global imbalance. And this is badly needed, because, despite the apparent complacency, there is still a vague feeling among policy-makers that the situation is unsustainable and that the US dollar will eventually need to fall further. Given the appreciation of European currencies against the dollar in recent years – and concerns that this would overtax the adjustment capacity of European economies – G-7 policy-makers have increasingly called on Asian countries, especially China, to allow their currencies to rise against the dollar. China's first step – a move towards a managed floating basket that involved an initial appreciation of 2.1% with respect to the US dollar – was encouraging, but this modest response despite the tremendous pressure exerted by US policy-makers shows how difficult it will be to achieve equilibrium only through price adjustment.

In fact, we doubt that exchange rate changes will suffice to restore current account imbalances to more sustainable levels. In our view, these imbalances are more deeply rooted in changes in the demand and supply of international savings which, in turn, have triggered important policy decisions in industrialised and developing countries. Adjustment will therefore not only require exchange rate changes but also changes in real interest rates and, along with these, probably in asset prices.

Specifically, we argue in this report that a rise in the international supply of savings from emerging market economies (EMEs) combined with a fall in investment in OECD countries pushed real interest rates to record lows. The deflation scare that emerged from the combination of the bursting of the stock market bubble, the shocks that ensued from the corporate scandals and geopolitical events, combined with the entering of

China and India into the world trading system, provoked in response a policy of aggressive lowering of nominal and real interest rates. An initial savings glut thus became a liquidity glut. While the fall in real interest rates was experienced in most OECD countries (and in particular in both the US and the eurozone), the impact on domestic demand was asymmetric and, consequently, current account imbalances rose. When the sustained increase in oil prices added to the savings-investment imbalance, current account imbalances reached historical highs.

Can this process continue? It is apparent that the US current account deficit cannot go on increasing forever, but our analysis suggests that even the current level is unlikely to represent an equilibrium in the long run as consumption is likely to increase in the oil-rich countries and investment is already increasing in most emerging markets. Both these developments should, in the medium run, restrict the global supply of savings available to fund the US current account deficit.

How does the story end? A few aspects seem clear.

First, there is little appetite for policy action, although there is a clear menu of policies that each player should be undertaking *for its own good* – namely, fiscal adjustment in the US, accelerated structural reform in Europe and exchange rate appreciation in Asia – yet none shows signs of taking these actions.[1] Thus, one should not expect any relief from the current constellation of policy-makers.

Second, although the cyclical mechanisms of adjustment are well understood, it is unclear whether there will be enough time to let them play out in practice. However, a confidence crisis in the US economy which would suddenly dry up foreign financing, make the dollar tumble and interest rates rise, remains a theoretical possibility, but the market's behaviour in recent years seems to suggest that it is highly unlikely.

Therefore, the most likely scenario remains one where the standard business-cycle dynamics play out, albeit in a very slow fashion. With investment recovering in OECD countries, we believe it is only a matter of

---

[1] In a similar fashion, the post-Katrina spike in oil prices in late 2005 generated a similar debate – and a similar non-response: in a world with very little spare capacity, higher oil taxes in the US and in Asia would be the obvious response to the demand/supply mismatch.

time before real and, ultimately, nominal rates rise. The rise in real rates – and the accompanying decline in asset prices – would in time rebalance domestic demand across regions and restore current account balances to more sustainable levels. This is likely to be the key adjustment mechanism, not changes in the bilateral euro/dollar exchange rate. If supervisors and regulators have ensured that the recent expansion in credit has been done under safe and sound criteria and there are no further shocks or policy mistakes, then the odds of a gradual and smooth adjustment are high.

Clearly, the longer one delays making gradual adjustments in the real interest rate and asset prices, the higher is the risk that the unwinding of the imbalances will impart serious exchange rate and asset price shocks on the world economy. While such a disruptive adjustment scenario may appear not very likely in the near-term future, we regard it as ever more likely the longer the present imbalances persist.

It is in this context that we ask ourselves whether the current framework for monetary policies around the globe is adequate. In a world with ever more integrated capital markets and global supply chains, the informational value of traditional domestic indicators of price pressures has declined significantly. Inflation is becoming a global phenomenon, and this raises the question of whether conducting monetary policy based on domestic Phillips curve considerations is still appropriate. We find a strong correlation between housing price inflation and current account deficits across developed countries, suggesting that, in the absence of wage inflation because of global labour arbitrage, overheating appears in the external accounts. Under this hypothesis, the US current account deficit and inflated housing markets could just be indications of an overheated economy, probably as a result of an overestimation of potential growth. Thus, it looks as if the global imbalance may not be a problem per se, but it could become one if it degenerates into excessive asset price inflation. A number of questions thus arise: Can a central bank consider its job done if it achieves internal balance at the expense of a large external imbalance? Should monetary policy be redefined as the achievement of financial stability in a way that encompasses internal and external balances, as well as asset price stability?

The answers to these questions provide the key to defining what the appropriate policy response should be. If the current global imbalance is simply the result of a combination of external shocks, then all actors must contribute to its resolution – and the euro area should try to stimulate its domestic demand to share the burden of the adjustment with the US, rather than considering itself 'in balance'. However, if the current global imbalance is a signal that the constellation of policies in the US is too loose, then the US should bear the brunt of the adjustment process – and the rest of the world should just admit that this US overheating has benefited them along the way rather than complain about the cost of the adjustment. We do not pretend that we have the answers to these questions at this stage. But by formulating these questions in a (hopefully) clear manner, we hope to improve the chance of finding the right answer when new facts emerge.

Introduction

As the US current account deficit has climbed beyond all previous historical records, concerns about the implications of this development and debates about possible remedies have intensified in academic and policy circles. Reference to the risks emanating from 'global imbalances' – which has become the politically correct synonym for the US current account deficit – has become a standard health warning accompanying most economic forecasts, and foreign exchange markets have repeatedly had the jitters. After a brief debate in late 2004, however, the excitement has waned: economic polices have barely changed and perceptions of the importance of the problem seem to be declining. In fact, the discussion has become largely politicised, with a different consensus emerging in each of the major economic areas of the world: the 'Washington consensus' blames China, the 'European consensus' blames the US fiscal deficit and the Fed's loose monetary policy, and the 'Asian consensus' sees the accumulation of foreign exchange reserves as an integral component of their managed floating exchange rate system. One consequence of these conflicting interpretations is a lack of any deep systematic analysis of the problem, since a large majority of the studies undertaken are intended to champion a specific agenda.

This report tries to fill this gap by providing a comprehensive discussion of the global imbalance. And this is badly needed, because, despite the apparent complacency, there is still a vague feeling among policy-makers that the situation is unsustainable and that the US dollar will eventually need to fall further. Given the appreciation of European currencies against the dollar in recent years – and concerns that this would overtax the adjustment capacity of European economies – policy-makers have increasingly called on Asian countries, especially China, to allow their currencies to rise against the dollar. China's first step – a move towards a managed floating basket that involved an initial appreciation of 2.1% with respect to the US dollar – was encouraging, but its small size despite the tremendous pressure exerted by US policy-makers shows how difficult it will be to achieve equilibrium only through price adjustment. In fact, we doubt that exchange rate changes will suffice to restore current account imbalances to more sustainable levels. In our view, these imbalances are more deeply rooted in changes in the demand and supply of international savings which, in turn, have triggered important policy decisions in industrialised and developing countries. Adjustment will therefore not only require exchange rate changes but also changes in real interest rates and, along with these, probably in asset prices.

Specifically, we argue in this report that a rise in the international supply of savings from emerging market economies (EMEs) in the late 1990s combined with a fall in investment in OECD countries in the early years of this decade pushed real interest rates to record lows. The deflation scare that emerged from the combination of the bursting of the stock market bubble, the shocks that ensued from the corporate scandals and the geopolitical events, and the entering of China and India into the world trading system generated a policy response leading to policy interest rates declining sharply in line with real capital market rates for capital. An initial savings glut thus became a liquidity glut. While the fall in real interest rates was experienced in most OECD countries (and in particular in both the US and the eurozone), the impact on domestic demand was asymmetric and, consequently, current account imbalances rose. When the sustained increase in oil prices added to the savings-investment imbalance, current account imbalances reached historical highs.

How does the story end? A few facts seem clear. First, there is little appetite for policy action, either at the domestic or the global level, although there is a clear menu of policy options that each player should be undertaking *for its own good* – namely, fiscal adjustment in the US, accelerated structural reform in Europe and exchange rate appreciation in Asia. None of the players, however, is heeding this advice. In a similar fashion, the post-Katrina spike in oil prices in 2005 generated a similar debate – and a similar non-response: in a world with very little spare capacity, higher oil taxes in the US and in Asia would be the obvious response to the demand/supply mismatch. Thus, one should not expect any relief from the current constellation of external imbalances by policy-makers. Second, although the cyclical mechanisms of adjustment are well understood, it is unclear how they would play out in practice. A typical crisis scenario, whereby eroded confidence in the US economy dries up foreign financing and makes the dollar tumble and interest rates rise, remains a theoretical possibility, but market behaviour in recent years seems to suggest that it is unlikely.

Therefore, the most likely scenario remains one where the standard business cycle dynamics play out, in a very slow fashion. With investment recovering in OECD countries, we believe it is only a matter of time before real and nominal rates rise. The rise in real rates – and accompanying decline in asset prices – would in time rebalance domestic demand across regions and restore current account balances to more sustainable levels. This is likely to be the key adjustment mechanism, not changes in the bilateral euro/dollar exchange rate. If supervisors and regulators have ensured that the recent expansion in credit has been done under safe and sound criteria, and if there are no further shocks or policy mistakes, then the odds of a gradual and smooth adjustment are fair. Clearly, the longer gradual adjustments in the real interest rate and asset prices are delayed, the higher is the risk that the unwinding of the imbalances imparts serious exchange rate and asset price shocks on the world economy. While such a disruptive adjustment scenario may not appear very likely in the near-term, we regard it as ever more likely as the forecasting horizon increases.

It is in this context that we ask ourselves whether the current framework for monetary policies around the globe is adequate. In a world with increasingly integrated capital markets and global supply chains, the information content of traditional domestic indicators of price pressures has declined significantly. The generation of inflation is becoming a global phenomenon, and this raises the question of whether conducting monetary policy based on domestic Phillips curve considerations is still appropriate. We find indeed a strong correlation between housing price inflation and current account deficits across developed countries, suggesting that, in the absence of wage inflation because of global labour arbitrage, overheating appears in asset prices and the external accounts. Under this hypothesis, the US current account deficit and inflated housing markets could simply be indications of an overheated economy, probably resulting from an overestimation of potential growth. If that is the case, the global imbalances may not pose a problem per se, but they need to be considered in the context of asset price changes and the role of monetary policy in connection with those changes. A number of questions thus arise: Can a central bank consider its job done if it achieves internal balance at the expense of a large external imbalance? Should monetary policy be ·redefined as the achievement of financial stability, in a way that encompasses internal and external balances, as well as asset price stability?

The answers to these questions provide the key to defining what the appropriate policy response should be. If the current global imbalance is simply the result of a combination of external shocks, then all actors must contribute to its resolution – and the euro area should try to stimulate its domestic demand to share the burden of the adjustment with the US, rather than considering itself 'in balance'. However, if the current global imbalance is a signal that the constellation of policies in the US is too loose, then the US should bear the brunt of the adjustment process – and the rest of the world should just admit that this overheating of the US economy has benefited them along the way rather than complain about the cost of the adjustment. We do not pretend that we have the answers to these questions at this stage. But by formulating these questions in a (hopefully) clear manner, we hope to improve the chance of finding the right answer when new facts emerge.

We proceed first, in chapter 1, by analysing the US external deficit on its own, pointing to some anomalies in the official data that suggest that both the deficit and the net external debt of the US might be worse than reported in the official statistics. Chapter 2 then sets the US deficit in the context of the global financial system, finding that its counterpart has recently been concentrated primarily in oil-exporting countries. Chapter 3 therefore explores briefly the reasons behind the increase in the price of oil and the future evolution of the demand-supply balance. Chapter 4 tries to fit the stylised facts of the major savings-investment imbalances that have developed over the last decade into the two main competing theories (labelled 'savings glut' and 'liquidity glut'). Chapter 5 concludes.

1. Is the US external position sustainable?

The single most eye-catching imbalance in the world economy today is the US current account deficit. Its counterparts are more or less sizeable current account surpluses in a number of other countries and regions. Given the unequal distribution of the imbalances, any analysis of this phenomenon must therefore start with a critical look at developments in the US current account. In this chapter we look at the US deficit from a purely national point of view, with a particular emphasis on the question whether there is any reason to expect a sudden loss of confidence in the US economy that might lead to crisis. We start with a brief description of how the deficit arose in the first place. We then discuss two sets of arguments that go in opposite directions. The first one focuses on the assertion that the US deficit is less important and actually smaller than suggested at first sight. The second argument focuses on two anomalies in the US external accounts that suggest that the official statistics actually do not properly track the huge external debt the US has accumulated so far. We conclude that markets are likely for the time being to focus on the first set of arguments, thus making the US situation sustainable. If markets were to focus on the anomalies in the official accounts, however, the stage could be set for a confidence crisis. Nevertheless, the probability of a balance-of-payments crisis developing in the US remains low, not least because of the large weight of the US in the world and the dominance of the US dollar in financial markets: there is simply nowhere capital could flee if investors lost confidence in the US.

1.1 How it came about

Over the last few years, the US current account deficit has gone from record to record, reaching close to 7% of GDP in 2005 (with the US merchandise trade deficit hitting a record high of $726 billion in that year, up 60% from 2001). Figure 1.1 shows that the external deficit has been trend wise increasing on any measure one could take (current account, net exports of goods and services or net real exports). Seen from a domestic, US point of view, the reasons for this widening gap are multiple, but can be summarised in one key point: domestic demand has increased on average each year by about half a percentage point more than output. What were the drivers behind this gap?

Since 2001, there has been a simultaneous increase in investment – as business spending on plant and equipment recovered from the recession and housing investment expanded further – and decline in national savings – as the sharp deterioration of the fiscal balance and the further decline in personal savings more than offset the improvement in corporate savings stemming from the restoration of corporate balance sheets. We show below that if looks back further than 2001, the decline in savings has been far more important than the increase in investment.

More recently, the income account has started to deteriorate, as expected, as the servicing of the huge net foreign liability position starts to weigh on the current account. We argue below that the magnitude of both debt service and the accumulated debt are probably significantly under-recorded. It is thus likely that, if properly measured, the current account deficit has actually deteriorated even further than officially recorded

Figure 1.1 The US external balance: Down by any measure

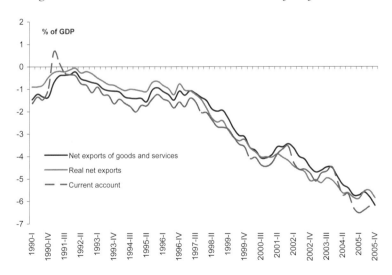

Source: Bureau of Economic Analysis, US Department of Commerce.

Box 1. Predicting the US current account

The US current account deficit has widened almost every year since the early 1990s. The year-to-year increase in the deficit increases was somewhat irregular, but usually less than 1% of GDP. The level reached now, over 6% of GDP for 2005, thus came about after a long, gradual process. *A priori* one would expect that such a long drawn-out process should be predictable, but this seems not to have been the case, at least if one looks at the forecasts of the IMF. Over the last seven years for which year-ahead projections of the World Economic Outlook (WEO) are available (1999-2005), the IMF has continuously predicted that the US deficit would be constant, whereas in reality it deteriorated each year, on average by close to $75 billion (0.7% of GDP) over this period.

Table 1.1 The US current account balance: Actual and forecast

	1998	1999	2000	2001	2002	2003	2004	2005
Actual data (1)	-214	-300	-416	-389	-475	-520	-668	-759
Forecast as of autumn of previous year (2)		-228	-308	-461	-446	-452	-583	-510
Forecast error (3) = (2) - (1)		-72	-108	71	-29	-68	-85	-249
Difference between forecast and actual data for forecast year (4) = (2) − (1)$_{t-1}$		-14	-8	-45	-56	23	-63	158
Difference in actual deficit (5) = (1) − (1)$_{t-1}$		-86	-116	27	-86	-44	-148	-91

Source: IMF, *World Economic Outlook*, autumn 2005 forecast.

It is interesting to note that the IMF made similar systematic forecast errors for the eurozone. But while the forecast error for the eurozone was of a similar size, it came about in a different way. For the eurozone, the IMF predicted almost continuously a substantial improvement in the current account (on average $50 billion), whereas in reality the eurozone's current account did not change much over this period. As a proportion of GDP, the forecast error for the eurozone was also close to 0.7% of GDP.

The role of the dollar exchange rate in this process of ever-increasing deficits seems to have been limited. In a first phase, from the mid-1990s to about 2000, the dollar appreciated along with an increasing deficit. As concerns about the size of the deficit increased, the US dollar then declined by about 15% from its peak in trade-weighted terms, but then recuperated part of the terrain lost in 2005, as US companies repatriated profits to take advantage of the Homeland Investment Act and as negative political news in Europe and Japan reduced the appeal of those currencies. The overall result of these ups and downs is that the US real effective exchange rate (based on unit labour costs) has appreciated only by a little (below 5%) between 1997 and 2005. This implies that it is difficult to argue that exchange rate movements have been a major factor behind the massive US deficit. Developments since 2000 are particularly difficult to reconcile with the view that the deficit is due to an overly strong dollar given that the US dollar has depreciated considerably in recent years on any basis one might take, but the US external deficit has continued to widen.

Partly for this reason, it is often argued that the US deficit is due to a growth deficit in the rest of the world. This argument is flawed, both on theoretical and empirical grounds. If the higher US growth rate were the result of a positive supply shock, one would expect that exports would increase – even at a constant or rising real exchange rate – along with the increase in the potential output. But this has not been the case: over the last decade, exports from the euro area have increased as much as exports from the US. Secondly, while it is true that growth in the eurozone and Japan has been disappointing, this has been more than compensated for by higher growth in emerging markets. Hence, it is not the case that the difference between US and *world* output growth has increased over the last decade. If one compares the ten years leading up to 1995 with the following decade, one finds that world output growth has actually increased slightly more than US growth (the US growth rate increased by 0.46 percentage points whereas world output growth – using PPP weights – increased by 0.53 percentage points).

It is thus not easy to explain the continuing widening of the US external deficit with the two main conventional factors: the exchange rate and relative growth rates. We will argue below that a key factor might have been that US policy-makers are overestimating the potential growth rate and are thus pushing demand above its potential, thus creating the gap between what the US produces and what it invests and consumes. This overestimation of the potential growth rate has apparently been shared by the international financial institutions, which explains why the continuous increase in the deficit was not anticipated, as analysed in Box 1.

The large increase in the deficit during 2005 does not necessarily imply that the process is accelerating. Timid signals of global rebalancing are becoming visible when one looks at the data more carefully. The deterioration in 2005 is due to a large extent to higher oil prices, and in fact the trade gap only increased marginally in real terms. In addition, growth in the eurozone and in Japan is starting to accelerate, as the impact of loose monetary polices is starting to be felt in those areas as well. Circumstances might thus be ripe for a reversal of the trend increase in the US deficit, but this evidently requires that domestic demand growth is restrained for some time. As we show below, whether or not this is the appropriate course of action depends crucially on how one interprets recent changes in global financial flows.

1.2   The role of offshoring

An important element of this rebalancing process is offshoring. We argued in Gros et al. (2004) that, once intra-company transactions are taken into account – that is, adopting an ownership definition of the current account – the US current account deficit would be reduced by about 1% of GDP. In addition, arguing that this portion of the current account deficit is less worrisome from the viewpoint of sustainability – why would a parent company default on its affiliate? – we concluded that, although funding remained a challenge, sustainability was less of a problem.

In a clear sign of globalisation at work, the correlation of exports and imports has increased dramatically, reaching over 90% since 2000 – compared to a long-run average of barely 50%. Pressing this argument further, it is interesting to notice that a portion of the US trade deficit is a necessary condition for sustained productivity growth. The argument is as follows: foreign affiliates typically follow two different strategies: market expansion or efficiency enhancement. Market expansion strategies typically have a positive effect on the current account, for the products manufactured abroad are usually sold in third-country markets. In addition, the higher profits represent a positive income flow for the current account. Thus, the net impact of this strategy is an improvement in the US current account.

Efficiency-enhancement strategies, however, have a very different impact. The home country exports parts to the host country, which manufactures the final product for sale worldwide – including in the home country. Thus, exporting parts and then importing final products (containing those parts) – that is, offshoring – leads to a deterioration in the current account. If the offshoring consists of services, instead of goods, then the export component is basically zero and thus the deterioration of the current account is larger. But crucially, this offshoring process is at the heart of the expansion of productivity growth, as companies seek lower-cost production centres, thereby freeing resources for higher value-added activities.

This strategy has two basic implications: first, this part of the deficit is key to sustaining high productivity growth, and it could be seen as desirable deficit; second, this part of the deficit is expected to expand in the future, going beyond manufacturing. For example, McKinsey (2003) estimates that the US business of IT and business processing offshoring in India will grow exponentially over the next few years reinforcing this process.

Figure 1.2 illustrates that there has been indeed a rather close correlation between US productivity developments and the current account deficit. The mid-1990s show a clear acceleration of productivity, which temporarily is decoupled from the current account, but over recent years the relationship is again rather tight.

Figure 1.2 US productivity and the current account

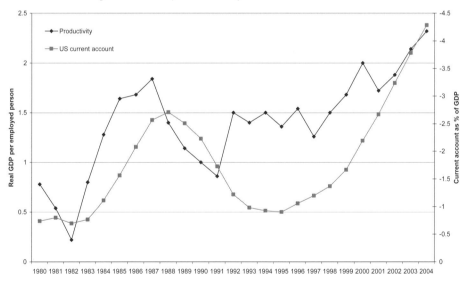

Source: Bureau of Economic Analysis, US Department of Commerce.

We return to this point later, when we argue that the absence of a hard external financing constraint has allowed the US to artificially boost its potential growth rate by moving resources from more mature sectors producing tradable goods to more dynamic sectors producing non-tradable goods and services. As we shall then see, this approach to raising productivity growth becomes unsustainable when the external financing constraint eventually kicks in.

Box 2. The impact of offshoring on the current account: An example

Let us assume that a PC sells in the US for $1,000. Let us examine what this transaction would look like from an accounting and an economics standpoint.

From an accounting perspective, the transaction looks as follows:

The screen, built in Taiwan, costs $400. The margin of the Taiwanese manufacturer is $40. The box, built in China, costs $150, with a margin of $10. The Intel chip (designed in the US but made by a Taiwanese company) costs $100 with a margin of $60 going back to Intel and $10 going to the Taiwanese company. The software costs $275, with a margin of $200. The profit for the US PC manufacturer is $75. Profits for the US economy are $75 + $200 + $60 = $335.

The profits for foreign economies are $40 + $10 (Taiwan) + $10 (China) = $60. Difference: + $265 for US companies. This is thus the essence of the business deal: US consumers get cheaper PCs and US companies capture most of the profits.

From an economics standpoint, however, the transaction looks as follows:

Imports: $925 (price of the PC minus the mark-up);

Exports: $275 (the software); Trade deficit= $640.

Increase in GDP, due to US companies' profits = $335.

Net loss for the US economy; $640 - $335 = -$305.

Thus, from an economics standpoint, what is profitable for US companies increases the external imbalance of the economy.

Why this apparent contradiction? Because US companies work with higher margins than foreign companies and they retain the higher value-added portion of the manufacturing process. Thus, if we were to compute the US trade balance with profits rather than with sales, the US would show a solid profit surplus.

1.3   Why sustainability might not be a problem: The role of net investment income and the currency composition of US assets and liabilities

A critical moment in the global imbalance discussion will be when the net interest income on the US net foreign asset position turns negative since this would signal a self-reinforcing deterioration of the US deficit. In the second half of 1998, the US net interest income was already negative, but the US dollar rally that ensued in the wake of the launching of the euro and the sharp decline in interest rates that followed the bursting of the stock market bubble led to a positive balance again, offsetting the impact of the ever-widening trade deficit. However, as interest rates increase and, more importantly, as the interest rate differential widens, the net income account should slowly turn negative and put additional pressure on the current account balance. When this happens, worries about the sustainability of the US position are likely to resurface strongly, as this negative balance will be a stark reminder of the explosive nature of the 25% of GDP net foreign liability position. In short, the higher US interest rates go, the worse the current account dynamics will become.

A critical feature of the US income account is that the US holds a net short US dollar position, whereby USD depreciation generates a positive wealth effect for the US. It is well known that the US has a net foreign liability position that is large and increasing. But it is less well known – although perhaps even more important – that the size of the gross positions has ballooned in recent years. US gross foreign assets rose from 30% of GDP in the early 1980s to over 70% in 2003, while US foreign liabilities skyrocketed from 22% to 95% of GDP, giving the 25% net foreign liability position.

In contrast to emerging market countries, however, developed countries typically hold foreign assets denominated in foreign currency and foreign liabilities denominated in domestic currency. In this case, currency depreciation increases the value of their foreign assets, thus generating a positive wealth effect. This short position on its own currency is a very convenient cyclical hedge, for currencies typically move in synch with economic developments – applying similar logic, the IMF has been recommending countries to issue debt indexed on their own GDP growth.

Estimates of this impact vary, but a good approximation is that a 10% USD depreciation improves the US net investment position by about 5% of GDP (Lane & Milesi-Ferreti, 2005, and Gourinchas & Rey, 2005). As cross-border investment activity continues, this effect will become even more important. If the US benefits from this wealth effect, who suffers from it? The counterpart of the US net USD short position is held by the Asian public sector and the European corporate sector, both of which are arguably overweight in US dollars – the Asian public sector through the perhaps excessive accumulation of reserves, and the European corporate sector as a result of the M&A frenzy of the late 1990s. Given that the negative wealth effect in Asia is absorbed by the public sector with no marked impact on the real economy, it is fair to conclude that the European economy is financing part of the US adjustment through lower profits and – probably – lower investment and job creation.

These unrealised capital gains also alter the view about the sustainability of the US current account position. The key to understanding the evolution of the income account is that, over the past 25 years, the rates of return on foreign assets owned by US residents and the rates paid on US debt owned by foreigners have been roughly equal for portfolio and banking investments. In contrast, the US return on foreign direct investment has on average been 6 percentage points higher than other countries' return on their direct investments in the US, while the return on US official investment has on average been 4 percentage points lower than official foreign investment in the US. In addition, the share of FDI and equity investment in US foreign assets is larger than that in foreign liabilities, and thus the US seems to have been taking higher risk in its foreign investments (see Lane & Milesi Ferretti, 2005). This explains why the United States has been able to maintain a net income surplus over the last 25 years, despite growing as a net debtor over this period.

Kouparsitas (2005) argues that assuming that the rates of return of the past 25 years will persist, the US could stabilise its current net foreign debt position by running a current account deficit of 1.3% of GDP. This estimate is still well below the current deficit, but there is an important caveat to note. The headline current account figures reported by the US Bureau of Economic Analysis (BEA) come from the national income accounts and they only include realised returns on foreign assets, while the BEA's foreign asset and foreign debt stock estimates reported in its annual net international investment position (IIP) take into account the unrealised capital gains from both changes in local currency prices and exchange rate adjustments. Given the net short USD position that the US holds, this is a key factor. Kouparsitas (2005) argues that the net effect of these price revaluations in 2003 raised the value of the net US IIP by 3.2% of GDP. If these unrealised gains were to be included as an item in the foreign income account, net US IIP would have been roughly 3.5% of GDP and the US current account deficit for 2003 would have been just 1.7% of GDP, roughly in line with the level that stabilises the external position. Corroborating this estimate, the actual change in the net IIP-to-GDP ratio was a decrease of 0.8 percentage points in 2003, well below the 4.8 percentage points implied by the current account as conventionally reported.

The common underlying theme of these considerations is that the imbalance could be less pronounced than the headline current account deficit suggests. However, it is important to understand that the wealth effect deriving from the USD depreciation is contingent on a constant USD decline – that is, for the US to be able to stabilise its external situation without adjustments to domestic demand, the USD needs to depreciate steadily in real effective terms so that the positive wealth effect offsets the deterioration of the debt-servicing needs. But should we trust the official data on which the above arguments are based? Probably not.

1.4   Why it may be worse than the official data suggest

The view that the US can run large deficits without accumulating an unsustainable external debt is based on the official statistics for the current account and the US international investment position. Closer examination of both reveals, however, a huge anomaly.

Over the last two decades, US residents have sold a total of around $5.5 trillion (thousand billion) worth net of IOUs to foreigners, whereas the officially recorded net investment position of the US has deteriorated only by a little over one half of this amount ($2.8 trillion) over the same period. The US capital market seems to have worked like a black hole for investors from the rest of world in which $2.7 trillion have vanished from sight – or at least from the official statistics.

How can $2.7 trillion disappear?

As argued above, it could be simply that the US makes large capital gains on its gross positions, because its assets are in foreign currency and its liabilities denominated in USD. However, the available data indicate that over the last two decades this factor netted the US at most $300-400 billion. This leaves a loss of over $2 trillion to be explained. The 'explanation' comes in two tranches of about $1 trillion each:

i)   Very large residual, 'other', or rather unexplained, changes recorded by the BEA in its statistics on the net US international investment position (IIP), which have averaged a similar order of magnitude.

ii)   An anomaly in the accounting item, 'reinvested earnings' in the balance of payments, which improves the US current account by about $50-$100 billon per annum because foreign firms report systematically very low profits for their US-owned operations.

These two phenomena, which must be kept separate, are explained below.

a)   The US as a black hole for foreign investment

We start with the second phenomenon, which consists basically of a huge stock-flow discrepancy. The stock, i.e. the net US IIP, should in principle be equal to the sum of past flows, i.e. current account balances (mostly deficits). However, this is by far not the case. Between 1982 and 2004, the US has accumulated a grand total of around $4.5 trillion of current account deficits. But its net international debtor position had deteriorated during the period 'only' by $2.7 billion (estimated at 'only' around $2.5 trillion as of end-2004). This implies a total of 'unearned' gains to the US of around $1.8 trillion during 22 years. Taking into account the balancing item 'errors and omission' does not significantly affect this conclusion since this item has summed to less than $250 billion over this period, thus leaving a hole of close to $1.6 trillion.

What can explain the approximately $1.6 trillion in vanishing deficits? The short answer is that this difference cannot be explained. It is as if the US capital market was a black hole: inflows disappear without leaving a trace. For a more detailed description of how this happens, it is necessary to restrict attention to a somewhat shorter period, for which more detailed data are available, namely 1989-2004. Over this 15 years period, the US cumulated current account deficits totalling $3.7 trillion, but its net IIP deteriorated only by about $2.5 billion. The lost capital thus amounts 'only' to about $1.2 trillion since 1989. Given the lack of detailed data for the period between 1982 and 1989 (the first period of large current account deficits), all one can say is that the US cumulated current account deficits of around $700 billion, but its net IIP (according to today's data) deteriorated only by $100 billion, leaving around $600 billion of unexplained gains.

These discrepancies are much larger than what one can observe for other countries. For example, Japan has accumulated current account surpluses worth around $2 trillion and its official net international investment position is very close to this amount. Gros (2006b) provides more detail for other countries as well as for the US.

Could the gain for the US be due to the fact that the US gains from a depreciation of the USD because most of its assets are in USD, but a large part of its liabilities are in foreign currency? Table 1.2 in Box 3 shows that this has not been the case. Over the period for which detailed data are available, exchange rate gains have totalled only around $220 billion. This is not surprising given that by end 2004, the US dollar was not far from the value it had already reached during the early 1990s.

Could the US have benefited from differential movements in stock markets? This is also unlikely *a priori* as over the long run the US stock market has not performed worse than its foreign counterparts. The table in Box 3 shows that indeed the sum of the net capital gains and losses over this time period was only around $120 million.

These two results imply that, even taking into account gains from capital revaluation, one cannot explain why the discrepancy between the cumulated current account deficit and the present net IIP of the US is so large. The table in Box 3 shows that over the last 15 years the sum of those changes in the US IIP that cannot be explained either by stock markets or by exchange rate changes is equal to close to $1.1 trillion.

What could be the reason for this discrepancy? The key to understanding the discrepancy (or the size of the item 'other changes') lies in the fact that the data on financial flows come from a completely different source than that on the net international investment position (IIP). The latter is essentially based on surveys organised by a number of institutions. The most important survey is the one that tries to measure foreign portfolio investment, i.e. US securities held by foreigners, which is done by the New York Federal Reserve. The size of foreign portfolio investment in the US is thus estimated on the basis of reports from US-based custodians, who are asked to detail the securities they hold on behalf of foreign owners. By contrast, the data on financial flows are based on the reports of brokers when they sell securities to foreigners. A share of a US company held by a European would thus not appear in the US IIP if the share is not held with a US-based custodian. But the purchase of the share would have been recorded in the balance of payments as a flow in the year the purchase took place.

Box 3. The US as black hole for foreign savings

The best (and only) background source for the stock-flow discrepancy is a recent tabulation by the BEA that shows the main sources of changes in the net US IIP (see below Table 1.2). The second column of this table shows for each year the financial flows that 'balance' the current account (minus errors and omissions, whose sum over this period was negligible). The last entry in this column shows the cumulated financial flows, or the cumulated current account deficits, whose sum amounts to $3.744 trillion over these 15 years. The last column in this table shows the net US IIP position at the end of each year. Comparing the beginning 1989 to the end 2004 value shows that the deterioration has been $2.553 trillion, approximately $1.2 trillion less than the sum of the current accounts. The explanation (or rather the lack thereof) lies in the columns (b)-(d).

Table 1.2 Components of changes in the net international investment position with direct investment at market value, 1989-2004 ($ billions)

Year	Position beginning	Financial flows	Changes in position Attributable to			Total	Position ending
			Valuation adjustments				
			Price changes	Exchange rate changes[1]	Other changes[2]		
		(a)	(b)	(c)	(d)	(a+b+c+d)	
1989	10	-50	7	-15	0	-57	-47
1990	-47	-60	-149	57	34	-118	-164
1991	-164	-46	-96	5	41	-96	-261
1992	-261	-96	-76	-75	55	-191	-452
1993	-452	-81	293	-22	119	308	-144
1994	-144	-127	23	73	40	9	-135
1995	-135	-86	-152	39	29	-171	-306
1996	-306	-138	84	-66	65	-54	-360
1997	-360	-221	-92	-208	58	-463	-823
1998	-823	-70	-288	68	41	-248	-1,071
1999	-1,071	-236	330	-126	66	33	-1,037
2000	-1,037	-486	134	-271	80	-544	-1,581
2001	-1,581	-400	-224	-152	18	-758	-2,339
2002	-2,339	-500	-60	231	213	-116	-2,455
2003	-2,455	-561	-2	416	230	83	-2,372
2004	-2,372	-585	147	272	-4	-170	-2,542
Sum totals		-3,744	-121	227	1,086	-2,553	

[1] Represents gains or losses on foreign-currency-denominated assets and liabilities due to their revaluation at current exchange rates.
[2] Includes changes in coverage, capital gains and losses of direct investment affiliates, and other adjustments to the value of assets and value of assets and liabilities.

Source: www.bea.gov. Data are consistent with those published in "The International Investment Position of the United States at Year End 2004", *Survey of Current Business,* July 2005.

Box 3, continued

Column c contains the exchange rate effect (most assets are in USD, but a large part of liabilities are in foreign currency). The last entry in column (c) in Table 1.2 shows that since 1989 the net gain from exchange rate changes for the US IIP has been only a bit over $220 billion.

Differential movements in stock markets seem also not to have been a major factor. The last entry in column (b) confirms that this is indeed not the case as the effect of the sum of the capital gains and losses over this time period has been to reduce the US net IIP by around $120 million.

The last entry in column (d) shows that over this period the sum of those changes in the US IIP that cannot be explained either by stock markets or by exchange rate changes is equal to close to $1.1 trillion.

Measuring the value of foreign ownership of US real estate is even more difficult (unless it is held for business purposes). The balance of payments would record the acquisition, but the surveys used for the IIP would have no way of accounting for it. It is thus apparent that the surveys will tend over time to miss part of foreign-owned assets in the US. However, as the BEA takes the surveys as the only reliable source for the US net IIP, it is forced to introduce the item 'other adjustments' in order to reconcile the data on the IIP with those from the balance of payments.

b) **Foreign direct investment in the US: Being taking to the cleaners?**

As mentioned above, a number of observers have noted two peculiarities of the US balance of payments: the first is that the US continues to report small positive net income flows although it has accumulated a huge foreign debt. The second is that the US, despite its undoubtedly large net foreign debt, is still reported to have a substantial net creditor position in terms of foreign direct investment (FDI). What is less widely appreciated is that these two anomalies are due to one, crucial item in the US balance of payments, namely reinvested (or retained) earnings (earnings minus repatriated dividends). On closer inspection, the flows reported for this item reveal an idiosyncrasy that suggests that it might be grossly mismeasured, thus distorting the published figures for both the US current account and its international investment position – the latter to the tune of a trillion dollars. Contrary to other contributors, we start from the hypothesis that it is unlikely that investors from all over the world would continue to pour hundreds of billions of dollars into FDI in the US if they had really been constantly taken to the cleaners.

The official data on reinvested earnings reported in the US balance of payments[2] cannot be taken at face value. This much is suggested by a simple comparison between the reinvested earnings reported on US direct investment abroad and those reported by foreign direct investment in the US – see Table 1.3 in Box 4. The former, i.e. what US firms report for their investment abroad, has amounted to over $1,100 billion over the last 20 years (1982-2004). The latter, i.e. what foreign firms report for their investment in the US, has amounted to less than $20 billion over the same period (on average less than $1 billion per annum)! It is difficult to accept this difference at face value, particularly since there is little difference in terms of distributed earnings between US FDI abroad and foreign FDI in the US and given that there is little difference in the reported returns on portfolio equity investment.

The purpose of establishing a balance of payments (BoP) for a country is to show how different kinds of payment flows balance, i.e. how inflows and outflows offset each other. Traditionally a balance of payments recorded just the payments made for the acquisition of goods and services or capital. Reinvested earnings were added relatively recently as a pure accounting entry to the balance of payments, although they do not represent a real flow of payments. They were added to reconcile the balance of payments data with the statistics on the international investment position, which is not immediately related to the flows of payments in the traditional balance of payments concept.

---

[2] The US data of course are also used in the statistics issued by international financial institutions (IFIs), such as the IMF.

Box 4. Being taken to the cleaners?

The fact that the official US current account does not show any substantial deficit under income flows has attracted a lot of attention. The US income account has not moved into deficit basically because the net return on FDI has been positive and increasing, thus offsetting the increasing net payments on bonds, on which the US has a very large debtor position. However, it has never been noted that most of the positive net income from FDI results from the huge difference in reported retained earnings. Table 1.3 below summarises the relevant gross flows. This table uses the average over longer periods because income flows tend to be variable from year to year. The table shows that more than one-half of the reported (gross) income from US direct investment abroad consists of retained earnings. By contrast, the (gross) income paid to the parents of firms with direct investment in the US consists almost entirely of distributed earnings.

On average over the last six years, the US has reported a *net* income from FDI of about $120 billion per annum.[1] Almost $100 billion p.a. of this is due to the difference in reported reinvested earnings and only about $25 billion to the difference in distributed earnings.

Table 1.3 Income on US direct investment abroad: Annual averages, 1999-2004
   ($ billions)

	Total reported profits (a)	Distributed earnings (b)	Reinvested earnings (c)=(a)-(b)
From US direct investment abroad	158.4	54.9	103.4
From FDI in the US	-38.9	-32.0	-6.9
Net US income	119.5	22.9	96.5

Source: BEA.

Eliminating retained earnings from the US current account would thus reduce the surplus of the US on direct investment income by almost $100 billion per annum (from $119.5 to $22.9 billion, thereby still leaving a small surplus). Given the deficit on portfolio investment, this implies that the US is in reality already now running a substantial deficit on the income account equivalent to almost 1% of US GDP.[2] For further analysis, see Gros (2006c).

---

[1] In 2005, this increased to $128 billion, but the precise split between retained earnings and dividend payments is not available yet for this year.

[2] As shown in more detail in BEA (2005), a switch between reinvested earnings to repatriated dividends (as occurred apparently during 2005) would also have other second-order implications for the current account, mainly through withholding taxes. But this would not materially change the results reported here.

Inserting the item 'reinvested earnings' into the balance of payments does not change the fact that the balance of payments always adds up to zero because reinvested earnings are entered twice and with opposite sign: for the foreign assets owned by home residents, reinvested earnings increase the income account part of the current account and then enter the capital account with a negative sign as an increase in direct investment abroad (and vice versa for foreign-owned direct investment at home). Reinvested earnings thus do not lead to any increase in errors and omissions, but they can change the way the balance looks: higher reinvested earnings make the current account look better and, over time, increase the value of direct investment abroad.

The fact that reinvested earnings represent a pure accounting entry has a key implication for how the data are collected. Since reinvested earnings do not correspond to a payment flow, they cannot be collected in the way almost all other entries in the balance of payments are collected, namely to rely on data from cross-border payment flows. Instead, in the regular surveys used to establish the US international investment position, US firms are asked to report the profits of their foreign affiliates. The replies are then combined with information on repatriated profits (actual payments of dividends, etc.) to calculate reinvested earnings, which are defined as profits minus repatriations. The latter correspond to financial flows that actually take place and can thus be cross-checked. But the former represent just the numbers reported by US parents of foreign enterprises. Higher reported profits abroad do not engender any additional tax liability (US tax is deferred until repatriation).

The same procedure also applies to US affiliates of foreign firms: they are also asked to report their profits. However, in this case the replies can be cross-checked with the profits declared by these firms, which are usually incorporated in the US. This difference in the meaning of the profits declared for BoP purposes suggests the reason why the US affiliates of foreign firms regularly declare rather low profits: to minimise their US tax liabilities.

Reporting profits to the US authorities has thus different tax implications for foreign direct investment in the US than for US direct investment abroad. A further indication that declared retained earnings are strongly influenced by fiscal and regulatory considerations is that during 2005, retained earnings reported by US firms on their foreign direct investment fell close to zero, compared to over $120 billion during the same period of 2004.[3] The changes in US tax regulations regarding the repatriation of profits earned abroad that were in force during 2005 thus had an immediate and strong impact.

These huge swings in the data should already constitute a reason not to rely on the accounting data used as the basis for official statistics. But there are also several other reasons for adopting a rather strong presumption that the rate of return on foreign direct in investment in the US should not be too different from the average return of US corporations (which in turn has not been too different from the longer run averages of dollar returns on major stock markets around the world).

The first reason derives from a simple comparison between FDI and portfolio investment. The official data imply that foreigners instantly start losing (compared to their US counterparts abroad) when they invest more than 10% into a US company. This conclusion seems unavoidable given that the rate of return on US portfolio assets has been the same as the rate on US portfolio liabilities (foreign investment in the US). Direct investment is any transaction under which a foreigner acquires more than 10% of the capital of an enterprise. It seems that foreign investors in the US are able to obtain a market rate of return (which can be objectively measured) if they own less than 10% of a US company. But the official statistics (based on accounting data) imply that their returns are much lower once the investment qualifies as direct, i.e. once it goes above the 10% threshold.

The second reason is that it is difficult to imagine that foreign investors would go to the trouble of making a direct investment in the US when there are much better profit opportunities at home. Apparently these opportunities have been exploited by US corporations, which report much higher profit rates. This would not only be a gross violation of the general assumption of market efficiency, but also of the general assumption that consistent profit opportunities will in the long run be exploited.

Finally, if the official statistics were correct, foreigners would accept a rate of return on their direct investment in the US of only around 2.5%,

---

[3] Before 2004, this item had mostly fluctuated around this order of magnitude. As will become clearer below, the much lower figure reported for reinvested earnings for 2005 has as its accounting counterpart lower reported FDI abroad for that year. But a difference in a flow of around $120 billion will not have a measurable impact on the reported stock of US FDI, which is at present more than 20 times larger.

which would be much lower not only of that on their US portfolio equity investment, but also lower than the 5.5% return earned on debt instruments. The official data based on accounting returns would thus imply a strongly negative equity risk premium (for FDI alone!).

Box 5. Transfer pricing

How could the owners of foreign direct investment in the US reduce their reported profits and thus minimise their US tax liabilities? The bulk of foreign direct investment in the US concerns large corporations and leads to 100% foreign ownership.[1] The foreign owner can thus shift profits easily in and out of the US. The key consideration about where to generate profits will thus be taxation. Since the US corporate income tax rate is higher than in most other countries, it follows that most owners of direct investment in the US have an incentive to shift profits from the US subsidiary level to the mother company or, even better, a holding company located in a tax haven.

One obvious means of shifting profits is via transfer pricing. By charging the US subsidiary a high price for goods and services delivered by the foreign mother company, profits could be easily shifted out of the US.

If transfer pricing had been the main reason for the low reported rates of return on foreign direct investment in the US, one would have to observe that reported export prices decline relative to import prices[2] – and the magnitude of this mis-measurement of the terms of trade would have to be large. As shown in more detail below, the profits declared by foreign direct investors in the US are on average around $120 billion (annually) lower than one would expect if they earned a normal profit rate on their investment in the US. Given that US exports are worth about $1,100 billion, this implies that the US terms of trade should be distorted by transfer pricing by 10-11%. If transfer pricing had an important impact on measured profits, one should thus observe a trend deterioration of the US terms of trade over the last few decades of about 10%. However, this does not seem to have been the case. The US terms of trade have fluctuated around a constant value over the last 20 years (in line with fluctuations in the oil prices) without any discernible long-term trend, as shown in more detail in Gros (2006c).

---

[1] This implies that for most of the FDI that actually takes place, the 10% threshold is not material. The US internal revenue service (IRS) treats foreign-controlled companies differently from domestic companies. Foreign-controlled is defined by the IRS as foreign ownership of 50% or more.

[2] For a given level of FDI transfer pricing to shift profits out of the US, the terms of trade might be constant, but the volume of FDI has been constantly increasing in recent decades – implying that a growing part of the US economy might be subject to this phenomenon.

Transfer pricing could be one explanation, but as Box 5 shows, this does not seem to be the case in reality. If transfer pricing had been the main reason for the low reported rates of return on foreign direct investment in the US, one would have to observe that the US terms of trade should be understated by around 10-11% (because foreign owners of FDI in the US supposedly sell their subsidiaries' inputs at inflated prices and get the output at artificially low prices).

In calculating the US balance of payments, it might thus be better to ignore the large surplus on retained earnings (e.g. by ignoring this item on both US direct investment abroad and on foreign direct investment in the US). If this is done, the US current account deficit worsens by $120 billion. Making this adjustment also for past years leads to the conclusion that the net US international investment position is at least $1 trillion worse than commonly believed.

In this section we have discussed two glaring anomalies in the US external accounts. Most other observers have taken the headline data at face value and marvelled at how the US was able to earn much more on its foreign assets than it pays out on its liabilities. We would argue that one should take the headline data with at least two very large grains of salt:

i)   The net US debtor position (IIP) is based on survey data that do not fit the data on financial flows. As the data on financial flows mirror quite closely the data for real trade transactions, we would argue that it is more likely that the survey data are wrong because they miss foreign assets held in the US, thus under-reporting the net debtor position of the US.

ii)   It is unlikely that foreign investors would continue to invest hundreds of billions of dollars in the US if they really earned only the minuscule returns they report to the authorities. Hence, the US current account deficit is likely to be even larger than officially reported.

Does it matter that the true US external position is probably even weaker than officially reported? The answer is that this depends on the perception of the US by financial markets. As long as the US is perceived as a strong and dynamic economy, the market is likely to view the official statistics as proof of the superiority of the US. The specific instances of market reactions to negative news show that this view so far is still prevalent.

1.5   Market reactions: How likely is a sudden drop of the US dollar?

Market behaviour regarding the global imbalance has been confusing, to say the least. Foreign exchange markets are famous for not being able to focus on more than one issue at a time, and thus their attention shifts constantly. After the focus in 2004 – probably induced by the US election cycle – on the US current account deficit, triggered largely by discussions during the IMF Annual Meetings and leading to the sharp decline in the USD, markets stabilised around the turn of 2005, after the new US administration reversed policy and announced a new focus on fiscal consolidation. At that point, current account deficit considerations became secondary, and markets have been reacting to cyclical divergences, such as growth and interest rate differentials. Thus, despite the argument advanced above about the negative relationship between interest rate spreads and current account deficits, markets have been assuming that a faster path of interest rate hikes by the Fed would be positive for the USD. Since then, the USD has appreciated steadily, on the back of a better cyclical outlook and a widening interest rate differential. Going into the summer of 2005, the political uncertainty in Europe regarding the referenda on the European Constitution became the focus of markets, and the USD returned to its role as the main, and perhaps only, world reserve currency. If the euro were to disintegrate, as some European politicians seemed to be suggesting, this would be a good reason for the USD rallying further against the euro. Thus, markets seem to have 'forgotten' the extent of the US current account deficit and started to focus on cyclical and political developments as the main driver of currency moves.

This complacent view of the smooth adjustment has often been challenged by a number of papers arguing for an imminent dollar crash – see, for example, Summers (2004). Several structural features, including the higher import elasticity and the higher level of imports as compared to exports, suggest that, unless there is a significant change in relative domestic demand growth and/or relative prices, the US current account deficit will expand indefinitely and thus the odds of a dollar crash are very high.

A missing element in these crisis scenarios, however, is a discussion of what the likely dynamics of the crash would be. What would be the trigger that could lead to such a crash? An interesting case study is the downgrading of General Motors' debt in April 2005. One of the typical scenarios advanced to justify the odds of a crisis is that there could be a sudden drop of confidence in the US asset markets that could lead to a capital outflow from the US and a sharp decline in the USD. In this vein, the downgrade of General Motors in April of 2005, one of the icons of US industry, could have been an example of the type of event that could lead to a confidence crisis in the US economy. It is thus interesting to study the market reaction to that announcement.

The reaction was broadly as expected, with one very important caveat: the weight of the US economy in current economic growth is so large, or at least is perceived as being so large, that markets reacted in a correlated fashion, as if this shock was a shock to the global economy, not to the US market. Thus, world stock markets collapsed, world bond markets rallied, risk aversion increased – and therefore corporate bond and emerging market spreads widened. The reaction of the USD was very interesting: it sold off against the euro and the Swiss franc – the currencies perceived as alternative store of value – but it rallied against emerging market currencies. It was thus a typical flight to quality where the US bond market – and the USD broadly defined – was perceived as a 'quality' market, despite the fact that one of its iconic companies was being downgraded. Since the first downgrade, another ensued: Ford Motor, another of the Big Three American auto companies, was also downgraded. The market reaction was similar to the first instance – compounded this time by increased stress in the credit derivatives market – i.e. a generalised increase in risk aversion and flight to quality.

Thus, a crisis scenario built on the 'sudden loss of confidence' trigger is, so far, difficult to validate given the market's reaction to events that would have been a good excuse to sell the dollar. The key to this behaviour is the fact that the global economy is so interconnected and US growth is such an important component of global economic growth, that doubts about the health of the US economy lead rapidly to doubts about the sustainability of global growth. An alternative scenario that has not yet been tested would be an inflation scare. Given the highly-leveraged nature of the US consumer and the strong pace of housing market inflation, an inflation scare that led to a sudden spike in long-term interest rates would raise doubts about the sustainability of the US economy. Nevertheless, the question remains: what would be the reaction of markets faced with this scenario? Probably, after a brief spike in long-term interest rates, fears of a collapse of the US consumer would lead to an inversion of the curve as markets start pricing in rate cuts in the US, and with it the flight to quality process would start again – probably in a synchronised fashion. Given the different elasticities, a global recession could perhaps help to reduce the imbalance in the US external accounts, as imports would decline much more sharply than exports. Changes in demand growth differentials, rather than exchange rate movements, could thus in the end be the main drivers of adjustment.

2. Changes in Global Financial Markets and the US Current Account Deficit

From the discussion in Chapter 1, we may conclude that recent developments in the US current account, however we look at them, are unsustainable. But before jumping to the conclusion that the brunt of the adjustment must be borne by the exchange rate, as many analyses do, it is important to understand the underlying causes of these imbalances. We take a look in what follows at the genesis of the problem.

2.1 Booms and busts in emerging markets as the primary driver behind increased world savings

Equity markets were booming in the mid-1990s all over the world on the back of expectations of intensifying globalisation and a revolution in 'information and communications technologies'. At the same time, emerging markets were becoming popular destinations for international investors, particularly as their markets were opening up and offering high-growth potential and attractive rates of return. But the boom experienced in emerging markets came to an abrupt halt in 1997, as a combination of lax fiscal policies, rigid exchange rates and rapid growth in consumption and investment led to widening current account deficits financed by large short-term capital inflows. Indeed, outside of Asia and Eastern Europe, foreign direct investment constituted a small share of the financing of the current account deficits. These were the classic ingredients that provoked the crises that occurred between 1997 and 2002.

The history of crises in emerging markets in the late 1990s and early 2000s is well documented and we won't dwell on it here. Our interest is in the adjustment in current account and fiscal balances that followed the crises and its implications for the world real interest rate and for global savings and investment balances. Shut out of international capital markets, forced to embrace tough IMF medicine and elect more conservative governments, emerging markets began adopting sound economic policies: fixed exchange rates were abandoned, current account deficits turned into surpluses, large primary budget surpluses were generated, short-term external debt was eliminated and the depleted stock of international reserves was replenished to record levels.

Figures 2.1 and 2.2 show the cumulated current account position of East European, Asian, Middle Eastern and Latin American countries.[4] From a cumulated deficit of $75 billion in 1995, emerging markets turned their current accounts into a sizeable surplus of $83 billion in 1999, as fiscal and monetary policy tightening improved public and private savings-investment balances. Since 1999, competitive currencies and high commodity prices allowed emerging markets to generate even larger current account surpluses, reaching $367 billion in 2004. In 2004, the current account surplus among emerging markets' oil producers reached more than $150 billion – or nearly half of the total emerging markets' current account surplus.

Figure 2.1 Emerging markets' current account position ($ billions)

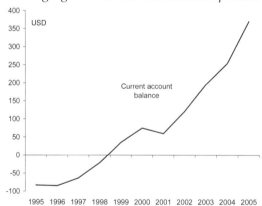

Source: IMF, *World Economic Outlook*, September 2005.

---

[4] The group of emerging market countries was built from IMF country groupings. Current account aggregates were computed by adding the current account balances in USD of these groups. The savings and investment ratios of our group of emerging markets was calculated as the weighted average of the IMF country groups on the basis of purchasing power GDP weights given by the IMF. The source of all data is the IMF's *World Economic Outlook* Database from September 2005.

Figure 2.2 Regional contributions to emerging markets' current account balances ($ billions)

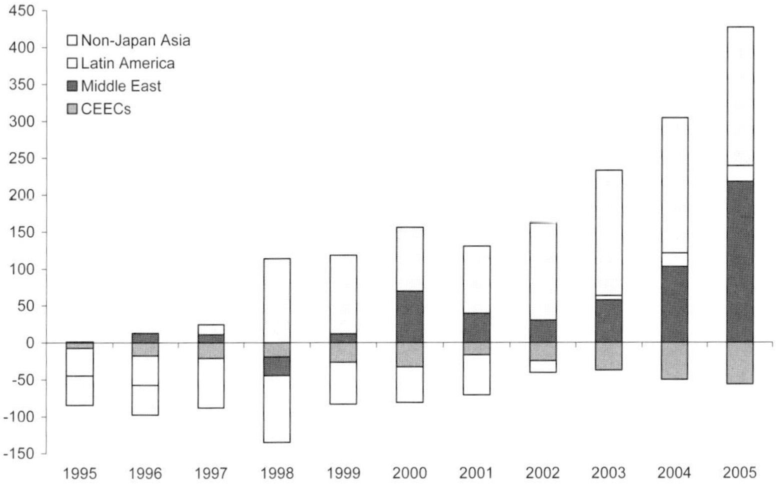

Source: IMF, *World Economic Outlook*, September 2005.

Figure 2.3 shows for the same group of countries gross national savings and investment relative to GDP (the difference between the two series indicates the group's external balance and thus its net export of savings). As crises in emerging markets unfolded in the second half of the 1990s, emerging markets slashed their investment spending sharply. In 1998, national savings also fell, as a number of countries plunged into severe recession. Thereafter, however, savings recovered on the back of domestic austerity policies, while investment followed only with a lag and at a more moderate pace. As of 1999, in a major change from past behaviour and against conventional wisdom of development economics, emerging markets began exporting large and growing amounts of savings to the rest of the world. In more recent years, exports of savings from emerging markets were boosted further by rising commodity prices.

Figure 2.3 Emerging markets' national savings and investment positions (% of GDP)

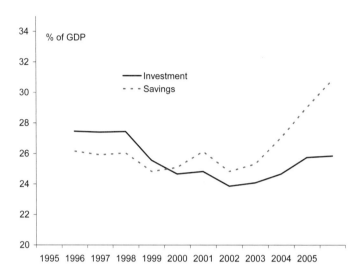

Source: IMF, *World Economic Outlook*, September 2005.

2.2 G-3: After the boom also the investment bust

While emerging market countries experienced balance-of-payment crises and stabilisation recessions in the second half of the 1990s, industrialised countries enjoyed an economic boom on the back of surging stock markets and euphoria about the benefits of new information and communications technologies. In 2000, however, the boom turned into a bust as the valuation of 'new economy' equities climbed to irrational highs. In the event, the equity markets decline triggered a sharp drop in investment, as companies struggled to repair their balance sheets by paying down debt, and industrialised economies fell into stagnation or recession.

Throughout the second half of the 1990s, industrialised countries had been net importers of international savings, reflecting a rise in investment on the back of the new technology boom that had not been matched by a corresponding rise in domestic savings. After 2000, however, investment in industrialised countries fell, just at the time when emerging market countries stepped up their export of savings (Figure 2.4).

Figure 2.4 Emerging markets' savings and industrialised countries' investment positions (% of GDP)

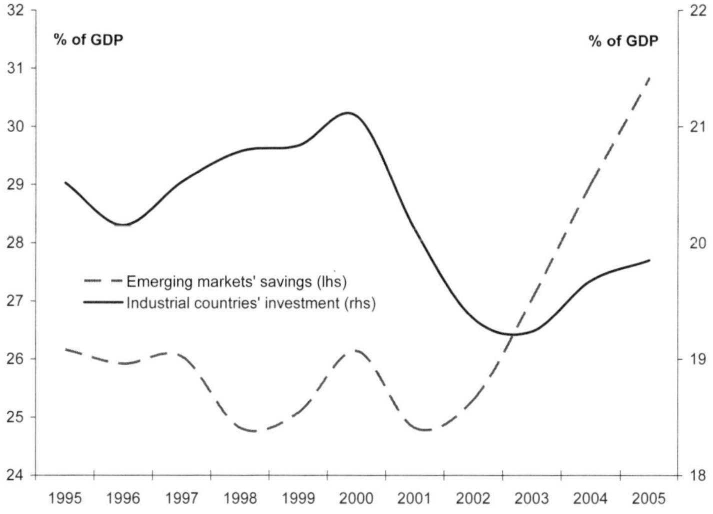

Source: IMF, *World Economic Outlook*, September 2005.

At the beginning of the new millennium, global capital markets therefore were suddenly confronted with a rising supply of savings from emerging markets and falling demand for these savings from industrialised countries, which were experiencing an investment recession. There was only one way to equilibrate the global supply of and demand for savings: global real interest rates had to fall (which then depressed industrialised countries' savings). This is illustrated in Figure 2.5, which shows the developments of the ratio of world investment-to-GDP and real US 10-year government bond yields, which we use here (somewhat loosely) as a proxy for global real interest rates.[5] The drop in investment (relative to GDP) in the industrialised countries (shown in Figure 2.4) pushed down the global investment ratio (as the rise in emerging markets' investment was too weak to compensate for the investment weakness elsewhere). As the investment ratio fell, real interest rates fell. As we argue in more detail below, the decline in real interest rates eventually helped turn around the decline in investment.

---

[5] To calculate real interest rates, we simply deflated nominal US bond yields with the US private consumption deflator.

Figure 2.5 Global investment and real interest rates

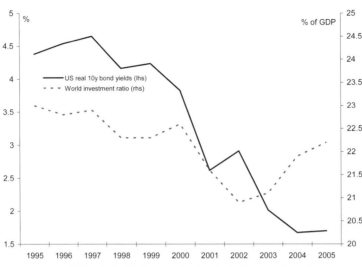

Source: IMF, *World Economic Outlook*, September 2005.

2.3 Effects on current account balances

A fall in global real interest rates was required to equilibrate the global market for savings and enforce the *ex-post* identity of real savings and investment. What was required was a new term structure of interest rates at a lower level, an exercise that involves the adjustment of both market and policy interest rates in a number of important markets, where exchange rate expectations interact with individual interest rate adjustments. Since interest rate response functions of policy institutions as well as financial market and economic structures differ across countries, the adjustment process evolves with trial and error, occurs at different speeds in different markets and is occasionally accompanied by considerable market volatility. A full description of this process with all details is impossible here. What is possible, however, is an analysis of a few key adjustment mechanisms and a discussion of the main implications of the interest rate adjustment.

Given their control over the short end of the yield curve, central banks played a key role in bringing real rates lower. Their reaction was prompted by the perceived shortfall of investment and excess supply of savings that threatened the economic outlook and raised the spectre of deflation. As central banks experienced these imbalances to different degrees at different points in time, and as their response functions differed, they adjusted interest rates by different magnitudes and speeds. Nevertheless, their main achievement was to stabilise inflation against the backdrop of the described changes in global savings and investment. As a result, nominal long-term rates fully reflected the fall in real rates, as shown for the US in Figure 2.6.

Figure 2.6 Nominal and real interest rates and inflation in the US

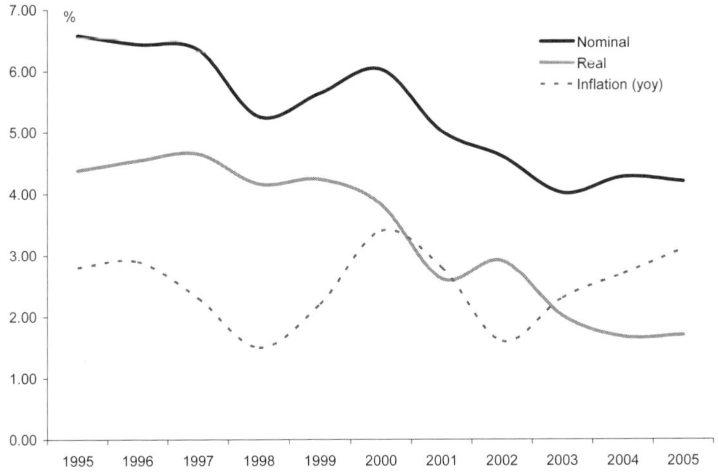

Source: IMF, *World Economic Outlook*, September 2005.

As discussed earlier, the decline in real rates was needed to balance the global demand and supply of savings. While the demand for savings by investors responds directly to changes in real interest rates, real and financial assets are the key channel of transmission for real interest rate changes to affect the supply of savings by private households in the industrialised countries.[6] With the decline in real interest rates raising asset prices, consumers felt wealthier and were inclined to reduce their savings.

The speed and magnitude of this link between asset prices and consumption are key determinants of the divergent reactions of domestic

---

[6] To illustrate this point, consider the following standard investment and consumption functions: (1) $I = I(r)$; (2) $C = C(Y,W(r))$. Equation (1) relates investment to the real interest rate and equation (2) relates consumption to income and wealth, which itself is a function of the real interest rate (with a decrease in r raising W).

demand to the global decline in real interest rates. Real estate markets played the most important role here given that housing still represents the most important asset for most families. Figure 2.7 shows how, in countries where housing prices increased strongly, real private consumption also grew strongly. Clearly, while the decline in real interest rates was a global phenomenon, demand and supply conditions in specific real estate markets mattered.[7] For instance, housing prices fell in Japan and Germany, where a supply overhang existed. Moreover, there are large regional differences even within countries. This applies *a fortiori* to the US, whose average value results from a property boom on both coasts, while prices seem to have moved relatively little in the centre of the country. Even in those European countries (much smaller than the US) where on average housing prices did not increase greatly, there were localised booms, with all the attendant wealth effects. In addition to the differential direct wealth effect of diverging housing price appreciation, differences in the equity extraction mechanisms across countries played an important role. In countries where refinancing is easy and not expensive, like in the US, or where mortgages are mainly at variable rates, like in the UK or Spain, the consumption boost from the appreciation of housing prices was magnified, exacerbating the external imbalance.

Figure 2.7 Housing prices (3rd qtr 2003) and real private consumption (2003) in 16 OECD countries

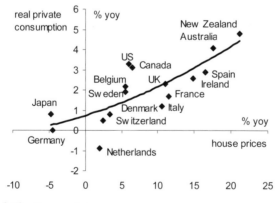

Source: OECD and *The Economist*.

---

[7] See Gros (2006a) for a more detailed description of housing price developments in the euro area.

Box 6. Spending on housing and the US current account

There can be no doubt that housing must have an important impact on household expenditure. One channel is via general consumption expenditure, which should be strongly affected given that two-thirds of households own the home they live in. Moreover, as a rule of thumb, families invest often 6-7 times their annual income in housing. This implies that a movement of housing prices of 10% can have a very strong impact on actual or perceived wealth. An increase or a fall in housing prices, of say 10%, could thus be equivalent to a gain or loss of more than one-half of annual income, with a correspondingly strong impact on demand for the cash-constrained part of the population.

It is not possible to isolate precisely the part of overall consumption expenditure that is due to housing wealth extraction, and expectations of future price appreciation might be as important as the level of house prices. A good indicator of how optimistic households feel about the prospects might be the level of residential investment. The figure below shows that there is indeed a strong correlation between residential investment (as a percentage of GDP) and the current account (again as a percentage of GDP). This close correlation constitutes another way to illustrate the likely link between the state of the US real estate market and the US current deficit.

Figure 2.8 US residential investment and the external deficit

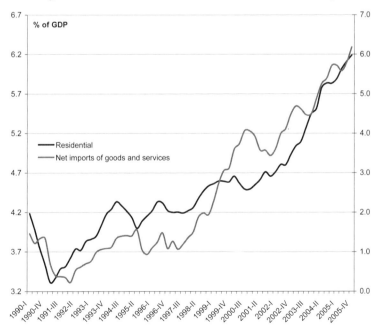

Source: Bureau of Economic Analysis, US Department of Commerce.

Fiscal policy also played an important role in restoring equilibrium in the global savings market. In particular, the US government turned from a net saver to a large dis-saver, absorbing a considerable amount of global savings and helping to stabilise domestic demand in the US. Other countries either had less room for fiscal policy manoeuvre or adopted a fiscal policy approach targeted to the long run, rather than to cyclical developments (this was largely the case in the euro area; see Gros et al., 2005), and were hence also less successful in redirecting savings (that were no longer needed to finance investment) to consumption. Countries with a lacklustre real estate market and little room for fiscal policy action had the largest adjustment difficulties. Germany and Japan are prime examples.

Through these mechanisms, national savings were eventually reduced in industrialised countries, allowing the latter to absorb the surplus savings of emerging markets at a time of lower investment activity, without triggering a major world recession. This was indeed an extraordinary achievement. However, as we argued above (and as Tables 2.1 and 2.2 below show), changes in national savings and investment were uneven across countries or country groupings, leaving the world with considerable international current account imbalances.

In sum, the stabilisation of the world economy at a time of huge changes in global savings and investment flows was accomplished through a large decline in real interest rates, which generated unpredecented current account imbalances.

As shown in Table 2.1, US gross national savings as a share of GDP fell sharply from its 1995-97 average to 2005, while investment remained broadly stable (thanks to the rebound in 2004 and 2005). The sharp fall in real interest rates, combined with an expansionary fiscal policy, contributed to these developments. As a result, the recession of 2001 remained short and shallow, but the national savings-investment deficit increased considerably (see Figure 2.9). Developments in the UK and Central and Eastern European countries (CEECs) were similar to those in the US (though of smaller magnitudes). In contrast, in Japan and the eurozone, the drop in national savings fell short of, or just compensated for, the drop in investment. Since consumption did not compensate for the fall in investment, growth in these regions trailed that of the US, the UK and Central and Eastern Europe.

Table 2.1 Changes in savings and investment ratios as a % of GDP (2005 relative to 1995-97)

	Savings	Investment	Change
US	-3.00	0.67	-3.67
Japan	-3.07	-4.37	1.30
Euro area	-0.37	-0.50	0.13
UK	-1.30	0.33	-1.63
CEECs	-0.37	0.13	-0.50
Emerging markets	4.80	-1.59	6.39
CIS	7.67	-2.67	10.33
Middle East	15.70	-1.70	17.40
Western hemisphere	2.43	-0.93	3.37
Asian NICs	-1.50	-7.00	5.50

Source: IMF, World Economic Outlook Database.

Figure 2.9 US savings-investment balances as a % of GDP

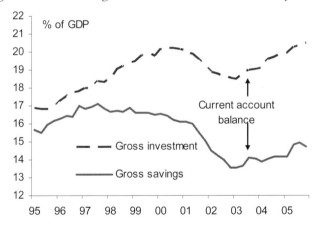

Source: DB Global Markets Research.

In most emerging markets (with the exception of the Asian newly industrialising countries, or NICs), national savings rose significantly between 1995-97 and 2005, while investment rose only little or fell. In the NICs, however, the savings-investment balance rose significantly because of the large decline in investment. As we argued above, this reflected in large part a change in economic policies aimed at reducing dependence on capital imports by creating a savings-investment surplus. In some regions, notably in the Middle East and the former Soviet republics forming the Commonwealth of Independent States (CIS), an improvement in terms of trade on the back of rising commodity prices added to the savings surplus.

In contrast to Japan and the eurozone, however, emerging markets managed to grow fast during these years as a result of strong export growth to the US and the EU. Many of these countries prevented their exchange rates from appreciating against the US dollar and hence fully benefited from rising US import demand. With private sector capital flows militating against an external savings surplus, countries had to intervene in the foreign exchange markets, occasionally on a large scale, to stabilise their exchange rates. Through this exchange rate policy, they effectively taxed consumption and subsidised exports, and turned their savings surplus into a rise in official foreign exchange reserves.

Table 2.2 shows changes in current accounts corresponding to changes in savings and investment balances. The current account position of emerging market countries improved by almost $450 billion between 1995-97 and 2005, while the current account position of the other countries/regions listed in the table deteriorated by some $700 billion. Within the latter group, the current account position of Japan rose while that of the euro area deteriorated. Thus, increases in the current account surpluses of emerging markets and Japan financed to a large degree the increase in the current account deficits of other countries.

Table 2.2 Changes in current account balances, 2005 and 1995-97 ($ billions)

	2005	1995-1997	Change
US	-759.018	-126.49	-632.52
Japan	153.101	91.23	61.87
Euro area	23.7	73.47	-49.77
UK	-53.854	-8.90	-44.95
CEECs	-56.4	-15.43	-40.97
Emerging markets	370.2	-77.2	447.4
CIS	105.3	-2.03	107.33
Middle East	217.6	8.23	209.37
Western hemisphere	21.3	-47.93	69.23
Asian NICs	78	2.03	75.97
Developing Asia	109.7	-24.10	133.80

Source: IMF, World Economic Outlook Database.

*Table 2.3 Current account balances and changes in real effective exchange rates,
2005 vs. 1995-97*

| | Current account balances ($ billions) | | | Change in real effective exchange rate |
| | Average | | | |
	2005	1995-97	Change	
US	-759	-126	-633	4.5
Japan	153	91	62	-27.5
Euro area	24	73	-50	-6.6
UK	-54	-9	-45	19.3
CEECs*	-56	15	-41	5.2
Emerging markets*	370	-77	447	-2.9
CIS	105	-2	107	
Middle East	218	8	209	
Western hemisphere	21	-48	69	
Asian NICs	78	2	76	
Developing Asia	110	-24	134	
Of which: *China*	*116*	*14*	*101*	*2.8*

* Change in real effective exchange rates for CEECs and emerging markets use the
difference between the years 2004 and the average of 1995-97.

Source: IMF, *World Economic Outlook*, International Financial Statistics and Direction of Trade
Databases, December 2005.

It is apparent from the last column of Table 2.3 that it is difficult to
attribute to exchange rate movements the massive shifts in current account
balances that have taken place over the last decade. The two entities with
the largest shifts in their external balance, the US and the group called
'emerging markets', experienced only marginal changes in their real
effective exchange rates, an appreciation of slightly under 5% for the US
and an even smaller depreciation for emerging markets. The same applies
also to the case of China, whose importance in providing a counterpart to
the US deficit is often overrated (as the table shows, China's surplus
increased 'only' by $100 billion against a deterioration for the US of over
$600 billion). It experienced only a marginal change in its real effective
exchange rate, which appreciated marginally over this period.

Box 7. Savings-investment = current account?

The attentive reader will have noticed an inconsistency between Tables 2.1 and 2.2. Table 2.1 reports that the deterioration in the US savings-investment balance amounted to 'only' 3.7% of GDP whereas Table 2.2 shows that the US current account deteriorated over the same period by over $600 billion, which as a percent of US GDP is closer to 5% than to 3.7%. In principle, the current account should be equal to the difference between (national) investment and savings (as assumed in Figure 2.9). However, this conceptual identity does not hold for the US. There is unfortunately an inconsistency between the US data for the savings-investment balance and the current account. The two tend to go together, over the medium run, but annual changes can differ considerably as shown in the scatter plot below, which shows the annual change in the savings-investment balance and the change in the current account for the last decade according to the official data (as reported by the IMF in its *World Economic Outlook*). It is apparent that the correlation is rather weak. The regression result from the trend line shown in the chart suggests that changes in the savings-investment balance variable can only explain less than one-quarter of the variation in current account changes (and the coefficient on the savings-investment balance is only 0.35, far from the value of 1, which one would expect).

Figure 2.10 Changes in US savings-investment balance and the US current account

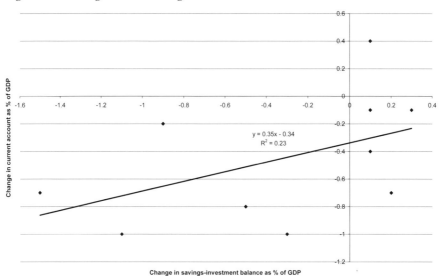

$y = 0.35x - 0.34$
$R^2 = 0.23$

Change in savings-investment balance as % of GDP

Source: IMF, *World Economic Outlook*, September 2005.

Box 7, continued

Is this inevitable because savings-investment data are derived from the national accounts whereas the current account data are derived principally from foreign trade statistics? This does not seem to be the case judging from what other countries report. The figure below shows exactly the same data for the UK. It is apparent that the UK data do not contain the inconsistency that one observes for the US. In the case of the UK, the equation explains 98% of the variation in the current account and the coefficient on the savings investment balance is almost exactly equal to one.

Figure 2.11 The savings-investment balance and the current account: The UK

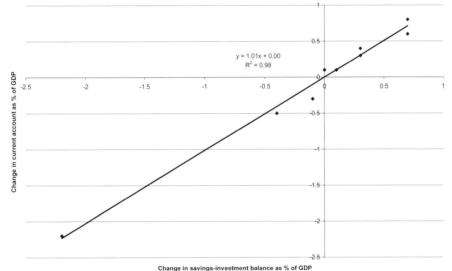

Source: IMF, *World Economic Outlook*, September 2005.

3. The Oil Price and the Sudden Emergence of Another Source of Excess Savings

In the last few years, another source of excess savings has appeared and grown very rapidly: the rising surplus of OPEC countries, documented in Table 2.2 above. This surplus is destined to grow even further in the current year as oil prices have stayed above their average 2005 level. The reason for the emergence of this surplus is quite simple: ever-rising oil prices transfer wealth from oil-consuming countries to oil-producing countries, and oil-producing countries have a higher propensity to save out of current income.

There are several reasons why OPEC and other oil-producing countries are not spending their windfall immediately. First, despite the existence of futures market pricing, there is considerable uncertainty about the future path of oil prices, and thus the marginal propensity to consume may be very low in the short run. Second, the international financial institutions (IFIs) are urging governments of oil-producing countries to build up stabilisation funds, advice that has been at least partially taken. This implies that governments are saving a substantial part of the windfalls that accrue to them in the form of higher royalties in order to raise national savings. These two mechanisms, both of which are based on the uncertainty surrounding future oil prices, are fundamentally very similar. We will return to this issue later.

A simple calculation can show that the magnitudes involved are significant. Around 50 billion barrels a day are produced by countries that are not themselves big consumers. An oil price increase of $30 a barrel (e.g. from $30 to $60/barrel) implies a transfer to these producers of about $1.5 billion per day, or around $550 billion per annum. If about one-half of this amount is initially saved, the increase in the oil price observed over the last year and a half is equivalent to a negative demand shock of about $250 billion for the oil-consuming countries. This alone would be equivalent to a drop in the investment ratio in both the US and the eurozone of over 1% of GDP. Under reasonable assumptions, the oil shock could thus have a significant impact on the global savings-investment balance.

3.1   A strong demand shock?

But are higher oil prices here to stay? The oil shock of the last few years indeed seems to be of a more permanent nature. During the 1990s, spot crude oil prices varied between $10 and $40 a barrel, but futures were stable at around $20 a barrel, signalling stability in the equilibrium price of oil at around this price. The last two years have witnessed a very different phenomenon, with a sharp acceleration of futures prices since early 2004 towards today's levels above $60 a barrel (see Figure 3.1 showing 2-year ahead future contracts). The futures markets are thus signalling that prices are expected to stay elevated, conferring on this oil price shock a more permanent nature. In order to understand the dynamics of recent oil price developments, it is fundamental to disentangle the shocks that have led to it. Current developments are a complex combination of supply, demand and portfolio shocks affecting oil markets.

Figure 3.1 Two-year ahead WTI* crude futures price

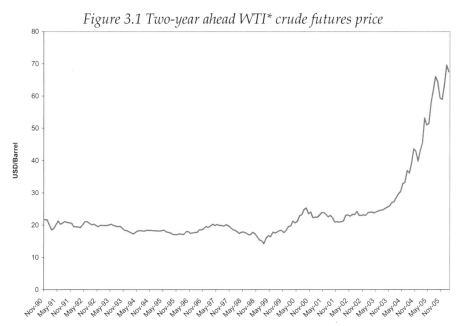

* WTI = West Texas International (a standard grade of crude oil).
Source: Bloomberg.

Demand growth has constantly been revised upwards over the last two years, as demand from emerging markets, especially from China which accounts for more than 40% of current demand growth, has been dramatically underestimated. Annual demand growth has increased over the past four years from 1% to over 3% in 2004. This increase in demand responds to a combination of factors, including higher economic growth, a sharp increase in the oil intensity of GDP of these countries as they adopt oil-consuming technologies, such as cars – Asia is projected to add 200 million cars in the next 20 years, a third of them in China – and an increase in strategic demand. The last two points are very important, for they represent a permanent shift in the demand curve that is much more inelastic with respect to prices. The shift in the demand curve can be clearly seen in Figure 3.2, where the relationship between oil inventory levels and prices has changed dramatically since 2004.

Figure 3.2 OECD oil stocks vs. crude prices

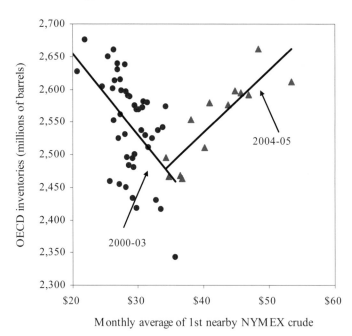

Source: OECD.

In fact, the replenishment of US strategic reserves accelerated in recent years, adding over 125 million barrels since 2002 – an increase of 25% – to reach the total storage capacity of 727 million barrels.[8] What is more relevant is that this increase represents almost one-half of 1% of annual production, not an insignificant number compared to the total increases in demand mentioned above. Note that these additions were all made in the context of rising prices, and an important contribution was made in 2004, thus adding to the marginal demand pressure against declining supply. Other countries are probably adopting similar strategies, and China has announced the creation of a strategic oil reserve. The rationale for all strategic reserves is ultimately an insurance against geopolitical risk. Therefore, geopolitical risk has been transformed from a risk premium worth a few extra dollars in the price of oil to an inelastic demand that is permanently increased. How long the governments of major oil-consuming countries will keep adding to their reserves remains therefore a major wildcard for the oil outlook. The debate may change in the post-Katrina era, as the evidence on the scarcity of supply – see below – may induce the authorities to relax the conditions for the use of strategic petroleum reserves (SPRs) across the world in an attempt to introduce two-way price risk.

3.2   A very tight supply situation

The response of supply has been very slow, to say the least. True, OPEC has been increasing production, but non-OPEC production has been sluggish. In addition, spare production capacity has fallen below 2 million b/d (and is probably now below 1 million b/d). Companies have not invested in new capacity in recent years, fearing a possible decline of prices towards $20/barrel and confronting the fact that remaining reserves are significantly costlier to extract than the mature basins the market is now draining. As an example, the lifting costs of the oil reserves in the US midwest – comparable in size to those of Saudi Arabia – is about $15/barrel, requiring prices of about $50/barrel to justify the investment required for extraction. By comparison, the lifting cost of Saudi Arabian oil is about $1.50/barrel. In addition, political turbulence in the areas that contain the

---

[8] The average price paid for this reserve is about $27/barrel. At current prices, this represents a potential profit for the US of over $12 billion.

cheaper available resources – not only in Saudi Arabia, but also in Russia and Venezuela, for example – is redirecting investment towards higher-cost and lower-return areas, compounding the problem.

A stabilisation of prices at around $35/barrel was seen by many companies as a precondition to resume investing, and thus the current outlook will provide a good test of this hypothesis. So far, oil companies have been returning cash to shareholders through share buybacks (for example, in 2005, Exxon bought back almost $10 billion and BP over $7 billion) rather than invest in new capacity. And this is taking place in a context in which spare capacity is at its lowest level in 30 years, with anecdotal evidence suggesting that it was almost 30 years ago when the last refinery in the US was built. In fact, refining capacity has fallen by about 10%, despite the sharp increase in gasoline demand.

Furthermore, geopolitical disruption risk to supply, both in the northern Persian Gulf – where all the spare production capacity lies – and in other producing countries and chokepoints, is higher and likely to remain so for the foreseeable future. The recent hardening of the stance of the US and EU against Iran only adds to this tension. Historically low spare-production capacity for an essential and strategic commodity like oil, with the United States *de facto* at war in the Middle East, should require a higher real price for oil.

In fact, the impact of Hurricane Katrina on oil prices in September 2004 reveals the overall perception of tightness of supply. Katrina knocked off 1.4 million barrels/day of Gulf of Mexico oil production, representing just about 2% of total world supply. Only 14 refineries were affected, accounting for a small percentage of total world capacity. Despite these relatively small numbers, prices spiked up in a major way, with oil prices reaching $70/barrel and gasoline prices increasing as much as 30% in Europe and the US. Stock releases of the US SPR and other countries' strategic reserves contributed to calm the jitters, and energy prices – with the exception of gasoline – had fallen back to pre-Katrina levels within two weeks of the event.

In fact, the impact of Katrina shows that over-consumption of gasoline is the real problem the world is facing. Even before Katrina struck, oil prices were elevated because of inadequate global refining capacity. The marginal barrels on offer, from Saudi Arabia and from the SPR, are mostly 'sour oil', which requires refining to become the light sweet crude that is in demand and that benchmarks oil prices.

Thus, in this context, a key policy question is how to rebalance gasoline consumption around the world. As Table 3.1 shows, despite being a global spot gasoline market, retail gasoline prices differ drastically across regions. Asian countries are heavily subsidising gasoline consumption while European countries are heavily taxing it, with the US somewhat in the middle. In a world where a probably long-lasting supply/demand imbalance is emerging, and where most of the excess demand is coming from Asian emerging countries, wouldn't it make sense to alter the incentives and eliminate the subsidies to gasoline consumption?

Table 3.1 World gasoline prices, August 2005

	Retail price/ gallon	Average world spot price	Retail - spot price
Europe			
France	$ 5.61	$ 2.13	$ 3.48
Germany	$ 5.97	$ 2.13	$ 3.84
United Kingdom	$ 6.02	$ 2.13	$ 3.89
Mean	$ 5.12	$ 2.13	$ 2.99
Asia			
China	$ 1.89	$ 2.13	$ (0.24)
India	$ 1.04	$ 2.13	$ (1.09)
Japan	$ 4.43	$ 2.13	$ 2.30
Mean	$ 2.44		$ 0.31
North America			
United States	$ 2.96	$ 2.13	$ 0.83
Mean	$ 2.77		$ 0.64

Source: Bloomberg.

A final important issue is that, as we emphasised above, futuresprices have increased in line with spot prices in contrast to other crude price spikes. In principle, this should mean that both demand and supply should react rather strongly to higher prices. This will be a key element in the longer-term outlook for the supply-demand balance discussed in section 3.4 below.

In fact, contango is a typical leading indicator of a decline in prices. The spread between the 1st and 2nd contract reached an all-time wide in spring 2005 and has remained elevated since then (see Figure 3.3).

Figure 3.3 Contango/backwardation and spot oil prices ($)

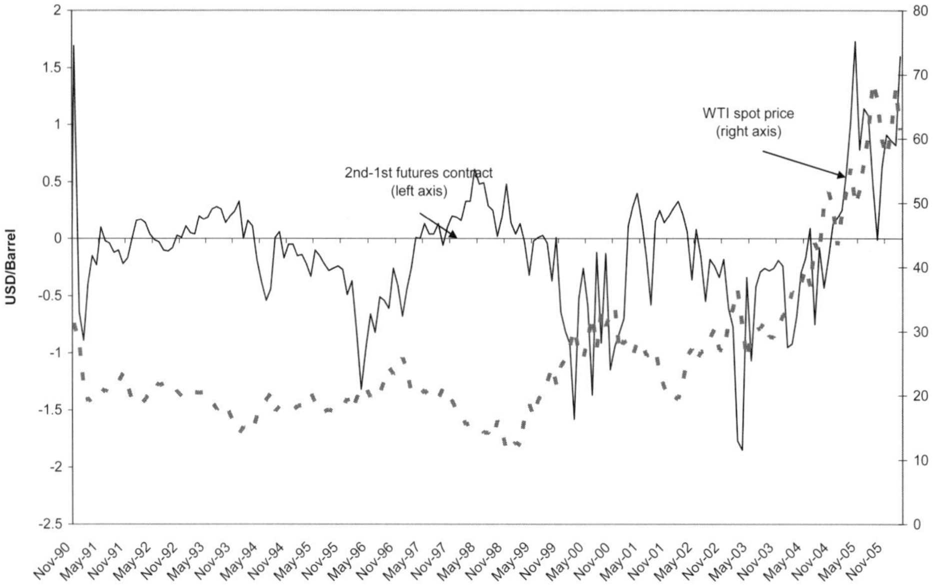

Source: Bloomberg.

Contango situations, like the one we are seeing now, have appeared historically when there have been ample physical oil supplies. The difference is that today's accumulation is largely voluntary, as market participants are accumulating 'excess' inventories as a precautionary action against a possible disruption of supply in a world with barely any excess capacity. As inventories swell, the oil prices move into contango, essentially discounting the price of the next-delivered barrel vs. oil delivered at a later date. This can be interpreted as a storage cost phenomenon: barrels have to be priced at a discount as cheap storage sites vanish. Potential producers can actually already today sell part of their future output at high prices. The same applies also to the demand side. Industries considering investment in energy savings will also be able to ensure that such investments remain profitable. In general, the higher long-term future prices of oil, compared to that of other energy sources, especially coal, means that the substitution of oil by other energy sources should be stronger than if future prices were much below the spot level. All in all, one would thus expect a rather strong medium-term reaction of both demand and supply to higher prices.[9]

3.3 An important portfolio shock

An important portfolio shock that exerts constant upward pressure on oil prices has added to the apparent discrepancy between demand and supply: an unprecedented inflow of capital into commodities as an alternative investment. That flow was largely precipitated by investment failure in other areas (equities) initially, but became self-sustaining. Long-only index strategies allocate a portion of resources to commodity indices, such as the GSCI and the DJAIG, seeking returns from price appreciation and the convenience yield of the forward curve.

Inflow into commodity indices has been very large: the compounded annual growth rate since 1991 has been over 30%, and about 50% since 2001. How big is this figure? A good yardstick is to compare it with the open interest of the relative futures markets. The capital in commodity indices owns about 40% of the crude futures open interest, 40% of the unleaded futures open interest, 40% of heating oil open interest and 25% of the natural gas open interest.

This inflow has two characteristics. First, it is long-only, with a trend-following strategy, whereby it is not likely to sell for anything less than a few years of bad returns. Thus, commodity indexation has taken on an autonomous life, and momentum investing is replacing the traditional portfolio theory: managers who entered the market early in the upswing are outperforming those who didn't, and increasing interest among pension fund managers is leading to self-fulfilling prophecies of commodity bullishness. The vast disparity between the sizes of the financial markets and the commodity markets is likely to cause painful dislocations in commodity-consuming businesses as investors distort the prices of some key commodities. For example, estimates of total retirement money in the US are at around $8 trillion, or about 60 times the size of the

---

[9] Econometric studies of the oil market typically use price elasticities on the order of 0.1-0.3 for both supply and demand (see Gately, 2004, and Gately & Huntington, 2002), but the permanent nature of some of these shocks would cast strong doubts over the stability of these equations.

entire commodity futures market. In other words, if 2% of retirement money were to move into commodities, the size of positions in the futures markets would double.

Second, arbitrage arguments explain why an increase in demand for front end futures can lead to price appreciation across the curve, thus causing the contango – back months being more expensive than front months – in the market. The argument is as follows: as we suggested above, long-only indexers seek to benefit from price appreciation and the yield of the forward curve. The convenience yield is captured by buying a deferred contract and holding it until some period prior to maturity, when it is rolled forward into another contract month. This strategy makes money if the forward curve is downward sloping, and loses money if it is upward sloping. The forward curve for physical commodities is a function of the cost and availability of storage, interest rates, short-term supply and demand dynamics and expectations for future price trends. Historically, crude oil tends to exhibit a pattern of becoming more backwardated – that is, the forward curve is more downward sloping – when prices rise, and less backwardated when prices fall. Thus, the current situation, in which the curve begins to slope upwards as prices rise, is very atypical. One reason for this structural break is the existence of this new class of long-only index investors: as the market has learnt their strategy of rolling forward the contracts to capture the convenience yield, markets have started front-running this roll-over, bidding up the prices of the more distant futures contracts, and thus the process of chasing higher prices has slowly become self-reinforcing.

Interestingly, speculative investors have not been behind the recent price volatility and major price spikes. A recent study by the Commodity Futures Trading Commission (Haigh et al., 2005) shows that hedging participants, including merchants, producers and refiners, change their positions often in response to market developments, leading hedge funds to change their positions in response. It is not a 'speculative bubble' that has led to the acceleration in commodity prices – in fact, despite a large fall in long speculative positions since mid-2004, oil prices continued rising – but rather a combination of fundamentals and new investment strategies.

3.4 The longer-term outlook for oil prices

We have emphasised so far that one key aspect of the increase in crude oil prices is that future prices have increased even more than spot prices. This is the case all along the curve, not only for deliveries a couple of month ahead, but also for deliveries years ahead as documented above. These forward prices imply that future spot prices should stay high. This can represent an equilibrium only if demand is expected to continue growing strongly despite higher prices and that supply does not react much either to higher prices (over the last years there has been no large 'exogenous shock' to supply, apart from temporary events, such as the usual spikes in Middle East political uncertainty). This scenario of continuing tight conditions in the oil market as far as the eye can see which is implicit in forward prices, is difficult to reconcile with the historical record. Over the last 15 years, demand growth has consistently oscillated around a value somewhat below 2% per annum (if measured over five-year intervals – see Figure 3.4 below).[10] The (spot) price had also, until 2004, fluctuated around a stable level of around $30/barrel (in real, inflation adjusted terms).

Is there any reason to believe that global oil demand growth will suddenly accelerate much above the trend (+/- 2% per annum) to which it settled down for about two decades after the price gyrations produced by the two previous oil shocks (1973, 1979)? It is unlikely that global growth will accelerate much over the next few years since global growth was already at close to its record in 2004 and 2005. But the weight of the faster-growing emerging markets is increasing (their growth rates are already at a record, but their weight increases constantly), and they are growing on the back of fast growth in industry and transportation, which are highly energy-intensive. Hence many argue that oil demand will be driven by emerging markets. This is at first sight an attractive hypothesis since over the last decade (a five-year horizon yields similar results), almost three-quarters of total demand *growth* has come from emerging markets (see Table 3.2 below). However, much of the increased oil (and generally energy) demand by EMEs might simply be due to the fact that manufacturing activity (which is energy-intensive) shifts from OECD countries to EMEs. Thus, the underlying increase in global oil demand may be lower than commonly estimated once the additions to 'strategic' oil reserves in the US and China (and possibly elsewhere) are taken into account.

---

[10] Before the late 1990s, consumption grew less (or was contracting) under the delayed impact of the 1980-81 price spike.

As an aside, one might note that there is indeed a marked difference between the EU and the US in terms of oil consumption: the US has been responsible for almost one-quarter of the global increase in oil consumption, against less than 10% for the EU. However, in terms of overall energy consumption (in the long run, different forms of energy are fungible), the difference between the EU and the US is much smaller, and can be entirely explained by the higher growth of the US. The image of a 'gas-guzzling' US with its SUVs against a 'thrifty' EU is correct if one looks only at oil, but in terms of overall energy consumption (or even more in terms of marginal energy efficiency of GDP), there is little difference, probably because of the higher share of industry in GDP in the EU.

Table 3.2 Partition of global increase in energy consumption, 1994-2004 (in %)

	Crude oil	**Primary energy**
Global total	100.0	100.0
OECD	37.2	35.4
of which: EU-25	9.0	9.6
US	22.5	13.5
FSU	-8.8	-2.5
EMEs	71.6	67.1

Source: BP, *World Energy Review*, 2005.

By how much would global oil demand growth have to accelerate so that the present level of prices represents an equilibrium? As a starting point, one can observe that the end-2005 price of around $60 per barrel represents roughly a doubling (in real terms) compared to the previous decade average. In other words, the question is whether a doubling of the price is needed to keep demand and supply in balance over the next decade.

Most studies of the oil market find a long-term elasticity of both demand and supply of between 0.1 and 0.3. Taking a value in the middle would imply that a doubling of the price (i.e. an increase of 100%) should lead to an increase in supply of about 20% and a fall in consumption (*ceteris paribus*) by a similar amount. *Ceteris paribus*, this implies that over the 'long run', let us say a decade, a gap of around 40% should open up between demand and supply. This would imply that demand growth would need to accelerate to around 4%, double the previous medium-term average for current price levels to be sustained.

Is there any reason to believe that the elasticity of oil demand has declined? The share of energy in general and oil in particular in GDP has actually fallen in recent decades and the price of coal, one important substitute for oil (at least in electricity generation), has not increased significantly. Both facts suggest that there is little reason to believe that the elasticity of demand has fallen. On the contrary, the relative stability of the price of coal means that the potential to substitute oil by other energy sources should actually be rather high – at least in emerging markets,[11] for the switching has already taken place to a large extent in OECD countries. The one element working in the opposite direction is that it is still difficult to substitute oil by other resources in transportation, and a quantum leap is taking place in this area in many emerging markets. However, transportation, while an important part of overall oil demand, still accounts for only about one-third of the total.

All in all, there is thus little reason to believe that the increase in oil prices observed during 2004 and 2005 will continue. In the medium to longer run, real prices are likely to stabilise and might even decline slightly if supply continues to expand as it has done regularly until recently. The big 'if' is thus the outlook for supply. Our analysis assumes that supply will behave as in the past and continue to be available to balance demand at current price levels (which reduce demand). The key question is thus whether the world will be able to find enough new capacity. There are many views (Matt Simmons' 2005 *Twilight in the Desert* being the most prominent) that argue that the supply curve is kinked so that the years of plentiful and inexpensive oil supplies are over and that the future holds a much more difficult and expensive search for new sources of oil capacity. If one considers, in addition, that the likely sources of new capacity are in the areas of the world where geopolitical risk is higher, the view that supply will be available at the same conditions as in the past has to be qualified to some extent. We do not wish to take a position on this issue. It is likely that the marginal cost of finding new sources of oil increases over time, but we doubt that it has suddenly doubled in the space of two years after having been roughly constant for decades.

---

[11] China is a case in point: here large coal reserves can satisfy most of the rapidly increasing energy needs of the manufacturing industry, but not of transportation, of course.

This analysis has two important implications:

At a stable (or slightly declining) oil price, one would expect that the savings rate of the oil exporters declines gradually as their consumption catches up to the increase in income. This happened rather quickly after the previous oil shocks, but the adjustment to higher income levels might be slower this time because most countries have learned from their mistakes and have created sizeable reserve funds.

If it is difficult to explain the doubling of prices along the entire curve with pure long-term supply and demand considerations. Other factors seem to have been at work. As mentioned above, there is some indication that the run-up in oil prices was linked to increased interest by financial investors. In part this reflected the increased recognition of commodities as an asset class, but it also may have reflected an increase in demand for commodities as an inflation hedge. There is thus some indication that the run-up in oil prices was at least partially related to the liquidity glut engineered by the G-3 central banks in their attempt to get their economies moving again.

Figure 3.4 Global oil consumption and real prices

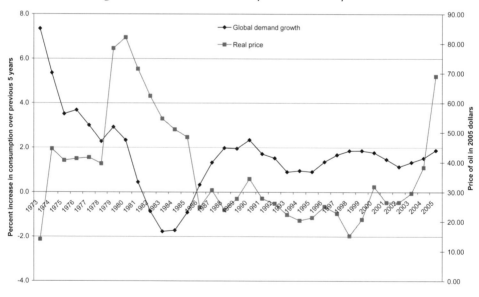

Source: BP, *World Energy Review*, 2005.

4. Theories to Fit the Facts

Our historical analysis of the phenomena of falling real interest rates and rising current account imbalances has given rise to competing theories about the fundamental drivers of these developments. Recognition of the latter is obviously necessary to design policies able to put the world on a course back towards equilibrium. In this chapter, we discuss two opposing views about the heart of the matter: the 'savings glut' and the 'liquidity glut' hypotheses.

4.1   Enter the savings glut hypothesis

In a speech on 10 March 2005, Ben Bernanke, then a member of the Board of Governors of the US Federal Reserve System and now Chairman of the Federal Reserve, pointed to a rising supply of international savings from emerging markets as a stable source of financing of the US current account deficit and the reason for low real world interest rates.

The excess savings story is by its nature difficult to verify (or disprove) because *ex post* savings must equal investment. But it might still be useful to describe the pattern of savings rates over the last five years, i.e. since the start of the decline in real interest rates (which coincides with the bursting of the internet bubble). We have described above the broad pattern of savings and investment rates of the G-3 economies. For this group of countries, the stylised facts seem to be as follows:

- In the US, savings collapsed after 2000, falling from 18% to about 13% of GDP.

- In the rest of the group of 'advanced economies' (as defined by the IMF's *World Economic Outlook*), savings rates stayed roughly constant.

The rest of the world, however, behaved quite differently. If one divides the rest of the world into oil and non-oil emerging market economies (EMEs), one observes that the savings rates of the oil producers vary sharply with the oil price. In 1999, their savings rate was under 26%;

for 2005 it has gone above 38%, an increase of over 13% of GDP between these two years. In the meantime, however, there were also significant swings in line with swings in the price of oil. The non-oil group in contrast has experienced a trend-wise increase in its savings rate from around 25% of GDP to around 32%.

Looking at investment, the data show much less variability: there is little difference between the US and the rest of the advanced economies (some increase towards 2000, some reduction until 2002 and near-full recovery by 2005). In the fuel exporters group, investment has fluctuated around 25% of GDP, with no discernible trend – but there is an uptick to about 27% of GDP in recent years. In the non-fuel producers group, investment is trending upwards, from around 25% to 30% of GDP (slightly less than the increase in savings).[12]

4.2   The savings vs. the liquidity glut hypotheses

The savings glut hypothesis sees high emerging market savings as the cause of low world interest rates, and regards strong US consumption as the main countervailing force against world recession. An opposing view – we call it the liquidity glut hypothesis – sees excessively low central bank interest rates as the cause of overpriced assets and persistent savings-investment imbalances. Whether present low levels of interest rates and current account balances are sustainable depends on who is right in this debate.

In his speech, Mr. Bernanke characterised the savings glut hypothesis as "somewhat unconventional". However, the core of his argument can be traced back to Karl Marx' theory of under-consumption. According to Marx,

---

[12] In the IMF's 2005 *World Economic Outlook*, world aggregates were weighted averages of advanced economies and EMEs aggregates, with the weights based on GDP at PPP (purchasing power parity). The aggregate series pointed to an increase in world savings over the last few years by around 1% of world GDP, but this was misleading: world savings have not increased if one sums national data in current dollar terms. The PPP-based GDP data give the EMEs a greater weight than if one were to just add current dollars. However, if one wants to examine the global savings/investment balance, the PPP weights are not appropriate since one dollar of net savings in China must offset one dollar of dis-savings somewhere else (e.g. the US), even if this dollar can buy many more haircuts in China than in the US.

the "original accumulation of capital" begins when subsistence farmers move to factories and are thus separated from their "means of production". The factory owners – the capitalists – pay their workers less than the value they create and use the difference to increase the capital stock. With wages depressed, aggregate consumption is low while savings and investment are growing fast. Reflecting the lack of final demand for the goods they produce, the capitalists ruin each other and monopoly suppliers emerge, until the impoverished masses overthrow the existing order.

Applying Marx' analysis of industrialisation in 19th century Great Britain to present-day developments in emerging market economies could lead us to conclude that industrialisation there is equally associated with under-consumption and a savings surplus. The key difference between now and then would be that excess savings in emerging market economies today are being used to finance US consumption. Thus, a new equilibrium growth path would emerge and capitalism would be saved from itself. But before we embrace this – let's call it 'new-Marxian' – analysis, we should note that Marx seriously underestimated the income and consumption growth of the working classes unleashed by industrialisation. In the event, capitalism thrived because it was capable of creating the consumers for the goods it produced. Hence, a savings glut does not necessarily follow from rapid industrialisation.

Another explanation for low world interest rates is a global policy of easy money. As emerging market economies industrialise and subsistence farmers become factory workers, the world capital-labour ratio declines. This exerts downward pressure on wages and consumer price inflation but raises the return to capital. In advanced economies, low wage competition from emerging markets may cause adjustment frictions which could depress aggregate demand.

Since labour is particularly cheap (and the return to capital especially high) in emerging markets, industrialised country companies are more inclined to raise investment and to create additional jobs there rather than at home (especially if they still see overcapacity there created during the last investment boom). With industrialised country growth sluggish as a result – and inflation contained by low-wage competition from abroad – central banks in these countries will try to support activity through a policy of low interest rates. Since business investment may not show much response, central banks will have to aim for an interest rate level low enough to stimulate private consumption and residential construction through rising real estate prices. In fact, the downward pressure on wages resulting from the emerging market economies entering the world trading system leads to a permanently higher share of wealth vs. wages in consumers' disposable income. As real estate prices and consumption react differently across countries to the interest rate stimulus, large current account imbalances are created and real estate prices may accelerate beyond fundamental levels.

The core of this argument has some resemblance to the so-called 'Austrian business cycle' theory, according to which business-cycle upturns are characterised by strong investment growth based on expectations of increases in productivity and returns to investment. But expectations may run ahead of reality and lead to over-investment and a misallocation of capital. This situation is exacerbated if monetary policy exploits inflation inertia and pushes the real financing rate temporarily below its 'natural' level (as defined by Wicksell). In the event, a fall in the return to capital and a return of the real financing rate to its natural level will lead to an investment downturn and recession, in which excess capacities are 'liquidated'.

Applying the Austrian theory to present-day events, we could argue that efforts by industrialised countries' central banks to prop up industrialised country investment through low interest rates at a time when more productive investment opportunities should exist in emerging market economies leads to over-investment and a mis-allocation of capital. When return expectations are frustrated or real interest rates move back towards their 'natural' level, investment will plunge and the economy will contract until the excess capacity is liquidated. Thus, what looks like a savings glut in new-Marxian analysis appears as an investment glut in the Austrian analysis.

The implications of these two competing explanations are very important. If the world economy is characterised by a savings glut emanating from emerging market economies, it may well remain in a stable (low interest rate) equilibrium as long as US consumers can be persuaded to spend and emerging markets continue to save. However, if world economic growth is sustained by excessively low central bank interest rates boosting real estate prices and current account imbalances to unsustainable levels, adjustment will sooner or later have to take place. The longer rates stay at abnormally low levels, the higher real estate prices climb, and the larger current account imbalances get, the higher the risk that adjustment will eventually be disruptive.

To provide a more structured discussion of the savings and liquidity glut hypotheses, it is helpful to express the theories in the context of a simple economic model. The following set of equations offers one possibility among others to do this:

(1) $S = I + (NAFA - NIFL)$

(2) $I = I(PA, OTHER)$

(3) $PA = PA(NAFA)$

(4) $NIFL = NIFL(r)$,

where S denotes savings, I non-financial investment, NAFA net acquisition of financial assets, NIFL net incurrence of financial liabilities, PA the price of (financial and non-financial) assets, OTHER other factors determining investment, and r the interest rate. With seven variables in this system of four equations, we need to determine three variables exogenously to solve it. An obvious choice is OTHER, but the selection of the second and third exogenous variable depends on how we interpret the savings glut hypothesis. Before we turn to this, let's first have a look at the equations.

The first equation is familiar from the national accounting identity equating national savings (S) to non-financial investment (I) plus net lending (NAFA-NIFL). In the case of an individual country, differences between S and I reflect lending to other countries, which gives rise to current account imbalances. Equation (2) relates investment to the price of assets and other factors (from which we abstract here). Following Tobin's Q theory, we assume that a rise in the price of assets induces more investment. The third equation stipulates that the price of assets rises with money spent on the net acquisition of financial assets while equation (4) relates net lending to the level of the interest rate.

To describe the savings glut hypothesis for the US in this framework, we assume NAFA and NIFL to be exogenous. A rise in foreign capital inflows raises the net incurrence of financial liabilities (NIFL). With net acquisition of financial assets (NAFA) assumed to remain stable, non-financial investment remains unaffected, but savings (S) and the interest rate (r) drop. Hence, we end up with a US current account deficit (reflected in a decline of NAFA-NIFL) and lower US interest rates. Clearly, Mr. Bernanke's implicit model was more sophisticated, allowing some feedback from lower interest rates to the acquisition of financial assets, asset prices and investment, but we believe that our simple approach captures the essence of the argument: a world savings glut creates a US current account deficit and depresses US interest rates.

But how can a world savings glut emerge and can the savings glut hypothesis also explain downward pressure on world interest rates? To answer this question, we restate our basic model for world aggregates. For the world as a whole, net acquisition of financial assets must of course equal net incurrence of financial liabilities and world savings must be equal to world non-financial investments – at least in theory, the world cannot run a current account imbalance with itself. Adding this constraint to our model gives:

(1') $\quad$ S = I + (NAFA – NIFL)

(2') $\quad$ I = I(PA, OTHER)

(3') $\quad$ PA = PA(NAFA)

(4') $\quad$ NIFL = NIFL(r)

(5) $\quad$ NAFA = NIFL

We now have five equations and the same number of seven variables, making it necessary to choose two exogenous variables. Apart from OTHER, there is only one sensible choice now: the interest rate r. Let's assume that there is a world central bank that can push r lower for exogenous reasons. As a result, net borrowing, i.e. NIFL, increases, pushing net lending (NAFA) higher by the same amount. Asset prices (PA) increase, raising non-financial investment (I), to which savings (S) adjust. Of course, OTHER factors may at the same time push investment down more forcefully so that a decline in r and a rise in NIFL, NAFA and PA can all go along with a drop in I and S. Clearly, when we restate our model for the world economy, we may again observe a decline in (world) interest rates and an increase in (world) savings, but causality from rates to savings now appears more sensible than from savings to rates (as we assumed in the one country case above). Moreover, other factors may well overwrite the relationship between the world interest rate and savings.

We have explained above how, in our view, central banks countered the worldwide investment downturn in the wake of the 2000-02 stock market crash by aggressively lowering interest rates, thereby boosting asset (and in particular real estate) prices with positive knock-on effects on private consumption. We also noted that the strategy was successful, with investment recovering in 2004, but admitted our puzzlement about the further decline in capital market rates in this economic environment.

All these developments can be more clearly explained in the above framework. The downturn in investment was driven by OTHER factors (i.e., the stock market crash) in equation (2'). In order to prevent the investment downturn causing a major recession, the US Federal Reserve lowered rates aggressively. Other central banks followed the expansionary monetary policy of the Fed to support their economies and to prevent a sharp appreciation of their currencies against the US dollar. With no signs of inflation, the cut of world central bank rates brought the world capital market rate r down. This boosted borrowing (4') and lending (5), raised asset prices (3'), and helped investment to recover (2').

There is no feedback mechanism in our model, however, from economic recovery to rates. An increase in rates depends entirely on the central banks' reaction to economic recovery. Assume that central banks target inflation and growth and that the world labour supply is augmented by incorporating workers previously occupied in subsistence agriculture in emerging markets into the world economy. As a result, the world capital-labour ratio falls, exerting downward pressure on wages and consumer goods inflation worldwide while raising the return to capital. In advanced economies, low-wage competition from emerging markets may cause adjustment frictions weighing on aggregate demand.

In this environment of low inflation and sluggish aggregate demand, central banks will keep official rates – and hence the cost of loanable funds – very low. This – and increasing profit margins – raises financial borrowing (NIFL) and asset prices (PA). World investment (I) picks up – with world savings (S) adjusting endogenously – and the world capital stock rises, gradually bringing the world capital-labour ratio back to a more normal level. Thus, low inflation, low interest rates, rising asset prices and increasing investment are all necessary features to accommodate the large increase in the world supply of labour due to the opening of China, India and other emerging market economies. Industrialisation in the latter may even imply a savings-investment surplus there when the move of people from farms to factories raises their productivity by more than their permanent income (and consumption) growth and the economy's ability to turn additional savings into productive investment is limited. Hence, what looks like a savings glut depressing interest rates may in reality be a rise in world savings and investment needed to endow additional labour with capital.

But not all investment is equally productive. Assume that business investment is more productive than housing investment and that companies want to increase the business sector capital stock primarily in emerging market economies, where the new, cheap labour is abundantly available. Assume further that the world interest rate is set by the G3 central banks (G3CBs) but, given their mandate, they focus primarily on domestic inflation and growth. In this case, G3 business investment may respond only weakly to low costs of borrowing (as G3 companies want to build up production capacities in emerging markets) and the G3CBs, aiming to support US investment, may push the world interest rate below the equilibrium level. The result would be excess borrowing and excessive increases in world asset prices, and possibly excess investment in low productivity capital, e.g. housing.

Following a sufficiently strong stimulus from low interest rates, investment (and GDP growth) may eventually pick up in the G3, inducing the G3CBs to begin withdrawing their monetary stimulus. However, with asset prices high (and for some asset classes possibly above fundamentally justified values), the central banks may feel that the change in the monetary policy stance should be implemented very carefully. Hence, they may want to signal markets that rates are unlikely to rise above a 'neutral' level, and that even the move to this level will be engineered very carefully. With the pace of official rate increases assumed by market participants to be 'measured' and the top of official rates seen tightly capped, term risk premia will be compressed and capital market rates will converge closely towards official rates. This is what we are presently experiencing: the Fed is slowly withdrawing accommodation, the ECB is following even more slowly despite excessive credit and money growth, and the Bank of Japan is only now preparing the exit from the policy regime of quantitative easing.

4.3   A few empirical observations

Rigorous tests of the two hypotheses against each other are hardly possible. What we can do, however, is check which hypothesis is better aligned with the facts. As mentioned above, there is no clear evidence of a rise in aggregate world savings. In fact, it seems that an increase in emerging markets' savings has been offset by a decline in industrialised countries' savings (once one uses the proper weights, see above). Figure 4.1 shows that indeed world savings have slightly declined, as a percentage of GDP, if one compares 2005 to 2000 (and the preceding years). With international capital markets fairly well integrated, the drop in world real interest rates is therefore difficult to explain by a savings glut.

Figure 4.1 World savings (as a % of GDP)

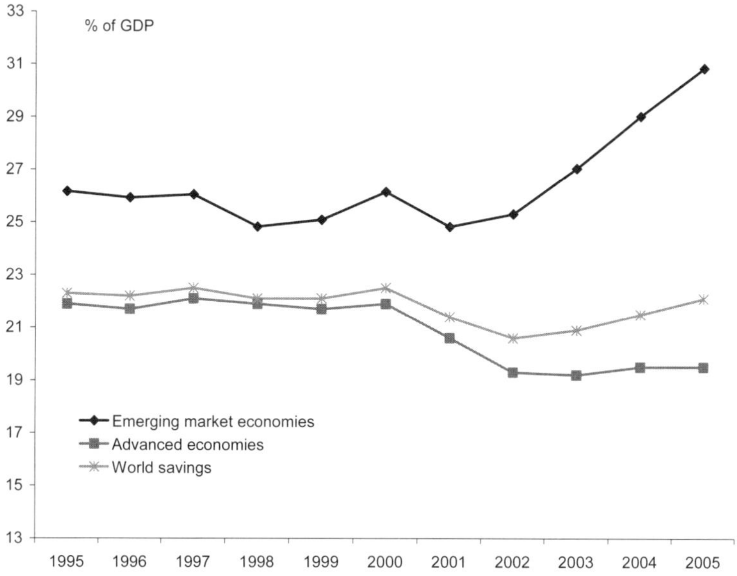

Source: IMF, *World Economic Outlook.*

Dooley et al. (2004) have argued that it is an increase in the internationally mobile – and not the total – supply of world savings that has exerted downward pressure on world interest rates. They see China as the source of the increase in international savings despite the fact that China still does not have an open capital market. In their view, the Chinese authorities have contributed to the emergence of a current account surplus by keeping the yuan low against the US dollar through massive exchange rate intervention, which by far exceeded the current account surplus because they also had to neutralise the impact of the equally large inflows of FDI and other, more short-term capital the country is receiving. However, China's net savings surplus is only part of the whole pattern of international current account imbalances. Taken on its own, savings exports from China do not seem large enough to explain the decline in world real interest rates (and the rise of the US current account deficit – see also Table 2.1 above).

Against this background, it seems to us that there is some evidence supporting the liquidity glut hypothesis. For one thing, risk premia in bond, credit, real estate and equity markets have been unusually compressed in recent years[13] – which has often reflected pressures from excess liquidity in search of investment opportunities. For another, world money growth has exceeded world GDP growth by considerable margins in recent years (see Figure 4.2). Finally, anecdotal evidence of speculative behaviour in real estate markets has been abundant, especially in the US, where former Federal Reserve Chairman Greenspan has characterised it as "pockets of froth in the real estate market".

Figure 4.2 Growth in GDP and money, 1984-2004

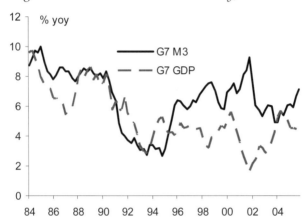

Source: Data for the US, Japan, Euroland, the UK and China.

In conclusion, it seems that the emergence of the savings glut in the latter part of the 1990s, combined with the post-bubble deflation scare, led central banks to create a liquidity glut that compressed risk premia and boosted asset prices. The challenge will now be to mop up the excess liquidity in an orderly fashion.

---

[13] See Alan Greenspan's recent speech in Jackson Hole, Wyoming (www.federalreserve.gov/boarddocs/speeches/2005/20050826/default.htm) where he makes explicit reference to the compressed risk premia in financial markets, which he had described before as a 'conundrum'.

4.4 The key factor behind the problem: The curse of the domestic Phillips curve

The key driver of world liquidity growth has been very loose central bank policy stances. Real short interest rates in the G3 have been very low for some time, mostly negative during the last three years, as the US Federal Reserve and the European Central Bank slashed rates to protect against the deflation scare and Japan entered a policy of quantitative easing to prevent a deflationary spiral. Faced with weak growth, low inflation and a weakening dollar, world central banks opted for a policy of easy money to insure against the downside risks to growth. In fact, despite its specific focus on money, the ECB has tolerated greater money and credit expansion in Euroland, relative to economic growth, than has occurred in the US, and real estate markets in several Euroland countries show considerable similarities with the hotter parts of the US real estate market.

However, the G3 central banks have operated under different conditions. The Bank of Japan (BoJ) has been trying to push the economy out of deflation and, with rates already at zero, a policy of monetary expansion has looked adequate. The ECB for a while was faced with an appreciating exchange rate, and thus a looser monetary policy that roughly offset the tightening induced by the exchange rate was appropriate. The key player remains the Federal Reserve. Faced with a depreciating exchange rate and a significant fiscal expansion, it still adopted a loose monetary policy, which was only corrected at a very gradual pace. Thus, the achievement of internal balance resulted in the deterioration of the external imbalance.

The key to understanding this development is that central banks determine domestic monetary policy on the basis of domestic conditions – i.e., the main driver of monetary policy decisions is the domestic Phillips curve, which is a function of estimates of domestic potential output. Thus, the important question is: should monetary policy be driven only by domestic considerations in an increasingly globalised world with global capital markets?

Presently, policy-makers seem to put US GDP growth consistent with low and stable inflation between 3% and 3.5%, in line with the trend increase of 3.2% during 1994-2005. However, while this rate over the last 10 years indeed went along with a fairly stable annual average rate of consumer price inflation of about 2.5%, it was accompanied by a rapidly widening external deficit. Thus, real net exports declined from -1.0% of

GDP in 1994 to over 6% of GDP in 2005, as real exports and imports grew at trend rates of 4.0% and 8.0%, respectively. Over the last 10 years, 3.2% trend growth of real US GDP was obviously consistent with low and stable inflation – and hence internal equilibrium – but it was inconsistent with external equilibrium.

In a small economy, such an inconsistency would not be sustainable for long. A rising external deficit would soon run into financing constraints, forcing the exchange rate down. A lower exchange rate would in the medium-term induce a reallocation of resources from the non-traded to the traded goods sector. In the short-term, however, it would probably trigger a rise in the price level. To counter a sustained increase in inflation, the central bank would need to prevent an easing of monetary conditions by raising interest rates to offset the effects from exchange rate depreciation. In the event, internal and external equilibrium would be restored.

In contrast to the small-economy case, the US faces only a soft external financing constraint. Rising current account deficits can be readily financed over a long period of time until foreign investors begin to lose their appetite for US assets and begin to worry about the debt-servicing capacity of the US economy. The lack of a hard external financing constraint over a protracted period of time allows excess demand in the US economy without noticeable inflationary pressures. Excess demand for non-tradable goods is satisfied by continuously moving resources from the traded to the non-traded goods sector. As a growing amount of resources is employed in the non-traded goods sector, demand for non-traded goods can be sustained at stable prices. Excess demand for traded goods can be satisfied at stable prices through rising net imports financed by capital inflows.

If technical progress raises productivity growth in the non-traded goods sector – as seems to have been the case in recent years – the reallocation of resources from the traded to the non-traded goods sector is even accompanied by an increase in measured trend GDP growth. A central bank concerned only with internal price stability will aim to keep growth in demand for non-tradable goods in line with the increase in their supply and be unperturbed by excess demand for tradable goods. The speed limit for monetary policy then is the rate at which resources can be reallocated from the traded to the non-traded goods sector. Especially in a fairly flexible economy benefiting from rising productivity growth in the non-traded goods sector, monetary conditions created by this approach are much too easy to ensure both internal and external equilibrium.

The accompanying Figure 4.3 shows three phases in the development of the ratio of value-added in the US non-tradable goods sector relative to the tradable goods sector since 1970. From 1970 to about 1981, the ratio remained broadly stable. In 1982, it began to increase at a steady rate (coinciding with the first period of large US current account deficits). Since 1995, it seems that the rate of increase of this ratio rose to a higher level. This is also reflected in the rising slope of the polynomial trend fitted to the raw data. Figure 4.4 shows that the increasing growth in the non-traded goods sector relative to the traded goods sector was accompanied by a higher current account deficit. Developments in the ratio of non-traded to traded goods sector valued-added correlate especially closely with the current account deficit since 1996.

Figure 4.3 US value-added (VA) in non-traded (NT) and traded goods (T) sectors (in current prices)

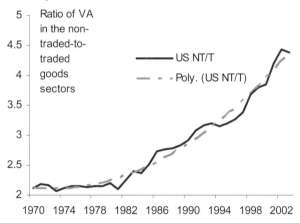

Sources: Deutsche Bank and OECD.

Figure 4.4 US non-traded-to-traded goods sector ratio and current account balance (% of GDP)

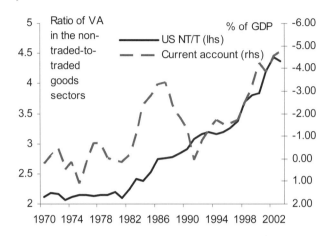

Sources: Deutsche Bank and OECD.

Figure 4.5 compares developments of the non-traded-to-traded goods sector ratio in the US to that of Germany. The latter country experienced a one-off jump in this relationship at the time of German unification (1990-95), largely driven by a rise of value-added in the construction sector. The increase in the German ratio of non-tradable to tradable value-added coincides with a sharp deterioration of the German current account until about 1995. From then on, Germany provides a mirror image of the US. As domestic demand falters after the end of the rebuilding boom in Eastern Germany, the traded sector expands whereas the non-traded sector contracts. The ratio stabilises and the current account improves steadily. This is consistent with findings of lower productivity growth in the non-traded goods sector, especially in retailing, in Europe compared to the US. Some economists have argued that this has been due to a lower increase in the use of information and communications technology in European retailing, probably caused by denser regulations reducing the intensity of competition. An alternative explanation would be that in a country with limited flexibility, it is simply difficult to shift resources between sectors. In Germany, for example, the non-traded sector was not allowed to shed labour at the same speed as its output contracted.

Figure 4.5 US and German value-added in non-traded vs. traded goods sectors (current prices)

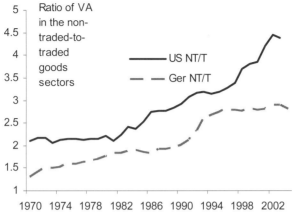

Sources: Deutsche Bank and OECD.

An infinite rise in the US external deficit is of course impossible, but even a stabilisation at current levels is not sustainable for long. However, there is no easy way to restore US external equilibrium. Conventional wisdom expects gradual dollar depreciation to solve the problem. This would indeed slow the trend of resource reallocation to the non-traded goods sector and probably also force the Fed to raise rates to compensate for the easing of monetary conditions through the exchange rate decline. In the event, US domestic demand growth would have to slow to reflect the more limited ability of the US economy to supply both traded and non-traded goods without additional foreign supply of traded goods.

For this to work, other countries would have to be able to adjust to exchange rate appreciation and the associated reallocation of resources from the tradable to the non-tradable goods sector. However, if their non-tradable goods sector is significantly less developed, or if adjustment costs are high due to economic rigidities, such a reallocation of resources could be accompanied by output losses. The former predicament may explain China's aversion to yuan appreciation, the latter, the aversion of Euroland authorities to the rise of the euro. In China, as in other newly industrialising countries, productivity growth in the traded-goods sector is much higher than in the non-traded goods sector. Hence, growth policy must create conditions for resources to flow from the non-traded to the traded-goods sector, which requires a relatively low real exchange rate. In

Euroland, resources laid off in the traded-goods sector may become unemployed rather than be re-employed in the non-traded goods sector. Hence, for these countries, currency appreciation may appear as a threat to growth and employment.

Therefore, if other countries resist upward pressures on their currencies and/or their efforts at structural reform are slow and incomplete, thus increasing the adjustment cost of the process, monetary policy will become too easy on a global scale. In the language of Dugger & Ubide (2004), the world is in a structural trap: cheap money becomes a substitute for reform, adjustment and hard policy choices. In an environment of readily available cheap labour, this may not raise world consumer price inflation in the near-term, but it is likely to boost asset and commodity prices, whose supply is more limited. Since international imbalances and the mis-pricing of assets are not sustainable forever, adjustment will eventually come, and rather abrupt exchange-rate and, especially, asset-price changes cannot be ruled out. This could include a sharp dollar sell-off and a drop in worldwide bond, real estate and equity prices (which have recouped most of the losses when an earlier stark overvaluation was reduced in 2001-03).

In fact, there is a positive correlation between current account deficits and asset price inflation. As Figure 4.6 shows, current account deficits are typically associated with housing price inflation above the long-term average, thus probably signalling some measure of overheating in the economy. Focusing on the external imbalance is thus akin to focusing on asset price inflation.

In this environment, monetary policy should augment its reaction function with a special attention to asset price developments. It is true that it is impossible to detect *ex-ante* asset price bubbles, but it is possible to detect anecdotes of asset price bubble-type behaviour. In the same way that central banks focus on pricing power anecdotes and credit developments to gain an edge over core inflation developments, central banks should focus on asset market anecdotes to gain an edge over asset-price behaviour. As asset prices react differently in different countries to similar monetary and credit conditions, policies will then be adapted accordingly. But interest rates are a very crude instrument to deal with asset markets, and thus a three-pronged approach to policy is needed: a combination of mild leaning against the wind with interest rates, supervisory action and regulatory tightening. This is the only way that the curse of the domestic Phillips curve can be overcome and dangerous financial excesses can be avoided.

Figure 4.6 Housing prices and the current account

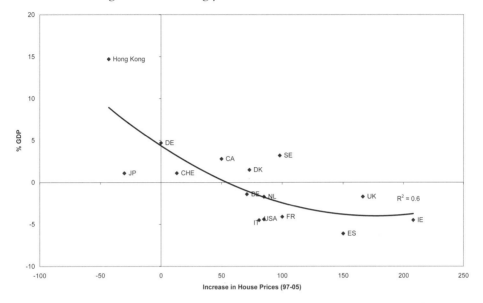

Sources: *The Economist* and IMF, *World Economic Outlook* database, September 2005.

In fact, this does not necessarily mean that asset price inflation must be avoided at all costs. As countries adopt different policy frameworks, their fundamental asset values – which reflect the expected discounted cash flow – will differ. If a growing external imbalance is predicated on fundamentally stronger domestic asset prices, then the imbalance is not necessarily a problem. With asset-related wealth becoming an ever-increasing component of disposable income, caution should be taken not to overreact to them. There is thus the need to focus on anecdotal behaviour to assess whether asset prices are out of balance or not.

5. Mind the Principle of Mean Reversion

With real rates at historical lows and current account imbalances at record highs due to the forces described above, we believe that we are approaching the phase when these variables will return to their historical mean. How mean reversion will occur is clearly the key question to answer. Conventional wisdom focuses on exchange rate changes and fiscal policy as the key channels for current account adjustments. Asian central banks' behaviour is also viewed as a key factor for interest rate adjustment. In our view, however, current account adjustment is likely to be driven by real interest rate adjustment, and the latter is likely to be determined by a shift in patterns of industrialised countries' investment and emerging markets' savings.

We briefly run through the conventional arguments. The extent of exchange rate adjustment required to bring the US current account deficit to a more sustainable level was recently estimated by Obstfeld & Rogoff (2004) to require an additional 20-40% trade-weighted depreciation of the dollar from its end-2004 level. The main effect of the dollar depreciation would be a rise of the price of tradable goods and services relative to non-tradables in the US, and a rise in the price of non-tradables relative to tradables in foreign countries. However, with many economies outside the US exhibiting only moderate degrees of flexibility, such large relative price changes, if not spread over a long period of time, would lead to severe economic frictions and substantial output losses. In the event, lower foreign income could depress imports by more than relative price changes would stimulate them. Hence, unless the process stretches over a very long period of time, US dollar depreciation alone would be unable to restore the US current account balance to a sustainable level.

What about US fiscal policy? Another popular argument – transferred from the 1980s – has been that fiscal retrenchment in the US would raise US national savings and hence reduce the US savings-investment balance and accompanying current account imbalances. However, while US fiscal deficit reduction may be important for the sustainability of US government finances, a recent paper published by the US Federal Reserve raises doubts about its effect on the external balance. According to Erceg et al. (2005), a drop in the fiscal deficit of one percentage point of GDP would induce the trade deficit to shrink by less than 0.2 percentage point of GDP. Applying this relationship to the current account suggests that the US government balance would have to shift from a deficit of 4.5% of GDP in 2004 to a surplus of 10.5% to reduce the US current account deficit from some 6% of GDP in 2004 to 3% in the future. This is obviously unrealistic.

Interest rate adjustment is also viewed as dependent on Asian central banks' continued willingness to accumulate US dollars and reinvest them in the US bond market.[14] As long as this recycling of Asian current account surpluses into US fixed income markets continues, bond yields can remain at a lower level than that warranted by economic fundamentals. In our view, however, while this is certainly an important part of the story, it does not explain it fully. First, the build-up of national savings in emerging markets has occurred earlier than the decline in interest rates and on a broader scale than only in the Asian context. It reflects a combination of factors that we highlighted earlier, including strict fiscal policies, high commodity prices and competitive exchange rates. Second, the current record low global real interest rate also reflected the bust of investment in industrialised countries. Moreover, there are limits to the willingness of Asian countries to accumulate assets in a depreciating currency, and of the US' ability to accumulate liabilities. At some point, creditor countries will feel that they possess enough foreign assets or, at a minimum, will slow the speed of foreign asset accumulation. Furthermore, the ability of central banks to contain appreciation pressures is increasingly being constrained by inflationary pressure and overheating (e.g. China and Russia). When that point is reached, current account imbalances will shrink from present levels.

But what mechanism other than changes in exchange rates, fiscal policy or Asian intervention policy could initiate the adjustment in real interest rates and current account balances? In our view, it is most likely

---

[14] This argument was put forward by Dooley et al. (2004).

sustained investment growth in industrialised countries coupled with an easing in emerging markets' savings surplus that will raise global real interest rates. Higher real interest rates, especially when they happen first and foremost in the current account deficit countries, especially, but not only the US, would raise savings and dampen investment in these countries. As a result, current account deficits would narrow to a level that can be sustained for a given real interest rate differential. In the event, global real interest rates would rise, but more so in countries with a current account deficit than those with a surplus, and current account imbalances would shrink in line with real interest rate differentials. Exchange rate changes and fiscal policy adjustment would contribute to the adjustment, but would not be the main driver.

Alternatively, adjustment could occur much more rapidly if asset prices – especially US real estate prices – collapsed. The immediate effect of a drop in US housing prices would be a plunge in consumption. This would, in turn, bring the stock market down along with investment. As the US economy would fall into a recession, the US dollar would drop. The exchange rate shock resulting from this drop would bring down growth in other countries, and the world would tumble into recession. As US domestic demand would have to fall by much more than foreign demand – and the latter would remain inherently weak – the world economic downturn could be vicious and deep until conditions are restored that allowed current account balances to be sustained again. In this environment, all but the safest assets would heavily lose in value, and the ageing population in industrialised countries, now stripped of their paper wealth, would see their pension provisions crumble.

6. Conclusions

In this report we have argued:

i)   However one looks at it, the US current account deficit is a serious and unsustainable imbalance, under-reported by official statistics.

ii) This imbalance has been created by a combination of rising savings surpluses in emerging markets, boosted in part by depressed exchange rates and exacerbated in the more recent past by the jump in oil prices, and a surge in world liquidity. The latter is the likely cause of the current low level of interest rates.

iii) US monetary policy has been a key supplier of world liquidity and may have contributed to the economy's external deficit by aiming for a trend GDP growth rate that is inconsistent with external equilibrium.

iv) The principle of mean reversion will reassert itself and bring external balances and asset valuations back to more sustainable levels.

A key question that remains to be addressed is how adjustment is likely to occur.

At present, the risk of a disruptive adjustment in the near future seems fairly low. First, emerging market countries may regard their non-traded goods sector as too underdeveloped to assume the role of growth engine presently held by the traded goods sector. For them, accepting a significant currency appreciation may seem tantamount to killing off this engine. Hence, they will try to prolong the status quo. Second, the sclerotic euro area economy may not allow the reallocation from the traded to the non-traded goods sector required for dollar depreciation to have the desired effect on external imbalances. European economic policies may therefore also be geared to support the status quo. Third, the present US Federal Reserve leadership does not seem very likely to take account of the need to restore external equilibrium in the conduct of its monetary policy. Also, fiscal retrenchment would not help if monetary policy would offset any negative demand effects to keep GDP growth at its elevated level inconsistent with external equilibrium. All this suggests that policy will do nothing to promote external adjustment.

What about financial markets? Clearly, the US dollar is in a long-term bear market. Markets seem reluctant, however, to push for the huge depreciation that academic studies have argued is necessary to restore external balance. Perhaps financial markets feel that exchange rate changes are unable to do the trick and hence are unlikely to assume the levels predicted by the academics. At the same time, there are no signs that asset markets are fostering adjustment. Bond and equity prices are reacting only mildly to the slow 'withdrawal of monetary stimulus' engineered by the Fed. The US real estate market, however, is starting to signal the beginning of a stabilisation process. How this process unfolds will be key to the health of the world economy. Perhaps the timing is optimal: as the EU and Japanese economies pick up strength, the world could undergo a smooth rebalancing whereby the US housing market slows down and with it the US consumer, being replaced by global investment and by EU and Japanese domestic demand that restores regional savings and investment imbalances to sustainable levels.

However, if we were only witnessing another false start, imbalance and mis-pricings would grow further until they have reached a level that triggers an endogenous implosion of the bubbles. The longer the status quo persists, the more likely disorderly adjustment becomes. The disorderly adjustment scenario could thus move from unlikely in the near-term to very likely in the long-term. Unless adjustment starts soon, economic policy-makers, financial market participants and ordinary citizens capable of looking beyond the near-term future better batten down the hatches and prepare for the perfect economic storm.

References

Bureau of Economic Analysis (BEA) (2005), US Department of Commerce, "How are the International Transactions Accounts affected by an increase in direct investment dividend receipts, such as those that may arise from the American Jobs Creation Act of 2004?" (available at http://www.bea.gov/bea/faq/international/ajca2004sum.htm).

Dooley, Michael, David Folkerts-Landau and Peter Garber (2004), *The Revived Bretton Woods System: The Effects of Periphery Intervention and Reserve Management on Interest Rates and Exchange Rates in Center Countries*, NBER Working Paper No. 10332, National Bureau of Economic Research, Cambridge, MA, March.

Dugger, Robert H. and Angel Ubide (2004), "Structural Traps, Politics and Monetary Policy", *International Finance,* Blackwell Publishing, Vol. 7(1), pp. 85-116.

Edwards, Sebastian (2005), "The End of Large Current Account Deficits, 1970-2002: Are there lessons for the United States?", paper presented at a symposium on The Greenspan Era: Lessons for the Future, sponsored by the Federal Reserve Bank of Kansas City, Jackson Hole, Wyoming, 25-27 August.

Erceg, C.J., L. Guerrieri and C. Gust (2005), *Expansionary shocks and the trade deficit*, Board of Governors of the Federal Reserve System, International Finance Discussion Paper No. 825, Washington, D.C., January.

Gately, Dermot (2004), "OPEC's Incentives for Faster Output Growth", *Energy Journal*, 25.

Gately, Dermot and Hillard Huntington (2002), "The Asymmetric Effects of Changes in Price and Income on Energy and Oil Demand", *Energy Journal*, 23(1), pp. 19-55.

Gourinchas, Pierre-Olivier and Helene Rey (2005), *From World Banker to World Venture Capitalist: US External Adjustment and the Exorbitant Privilege*, CEPR Discussion Paper Series, No. 5220, Centre for Economic Policy Research, London.

Greenspan, Alan (2005), "Reflections on central banking", speech at a symposium sponsored by the Federal Reserve Bank of Kansas City, Jackson Hole, Wyoming, 26 August.

Gros, Daniel, Thomas Mayer, Angel Ubide and Roberto Perotti (2004), *Breaking the Reform Deadlock*, 6th Annual Report of the CEPS Macroeconomic Policy Group, Centre for European Policy Studies (CEPS), Brussels.

Gros, Daniel, Thomas Mayer and Angel Ubide (2005), *EMU at Risk*, 7th Annual Report of the CEPS Macroeconomic Policy Group, Centre for European Policy Studies, Brussels.

Gros, Daniel (2006a), *Bubbles in real estate? A Long-Term Comparative Analysis of Housing Prices in Europe and the US"*, CEPS Working Document No. 239, Centre for European Policy Studies, Brussels.

Gros, Daniel (2006b), *Foreign investment in the US (I): Disappearing in a black hole?*, CEPS Working Document No. 242, Centre for European Policy Studies, Brussels.

Gros, Daniel (2006c), *Foreign investment in the US (II): Being taken to the cleaners?"*, CEPS Working Document No. 243, Centre for European Policy Studies, Brussels.

Haigh, Michael, Jana Hranaiova, and James Overdahl (2005), *Price dynamics, price discovery and large futures trader interactions in the energy complex*, Staff Research Report, Commodity Futures Trading Commission, Washington, D.C.

Issing, Otmar (2005), "Addressing global imbalances: The role of macroeconomic policy", contribution to the Banque de France Symposium on Productivity, Competitiveness and Globalisation, 31 October.

Kouparsitas, Michael (2005), Is the U.S. current account sustainable?, *Chicago Fed Letter*, No. 215, Federal Reserve Bank of Chicago, Chicago, Il.

Lane, Philip and Gian Maria Milesi-Ferretti (2005), *A Global Perspective on External Relations*, IMF Working Paper No. WP/05/161, IMF, Washington, D.C.

McKinsey (2003), *New horizons: Multinational company investment in developing economies*, McKinsey Global Institute, October.

Obstfeld, Maurice and Kenneth Rogoff (2004), *The unsustainable US current account position revisited*, NBER Working Paper 108969, National Bureau of Economic Research, Cambridge, MA, October.

Simmons, Matthew R. (2005), *Twilight in the Desert - The Coming Saudi Oil Shock and the World Economy*, New Jersey: John Wiley & Sons.

Summers, Lawrence H. (2004), "The US current account deficit and the global economy", Per Jacobson Lecture.

CEPS Macroeconomic Policy Group Reports, 1995-2005

EMU at Risk, Daniel Gros, Thomas Mayer and Angel Ubide, 7th Annual Report of the CEPS Macroeconomic Policy Group, June 2005

Breaking the Reform Deadlock, 6th Annual Report of the CEPS Macroeconomic Policy Group, Daniel Gros, Thomas Mayer and Angel Ubide, July 2004

The Nine Lives of the Stability Pact, Special Report of the CEPS Macroeconomic Policy Group, Daniel Gros, Thomas Mayer and Angel Ubide, February 2004

Adjusting to Leaner Times, 5th Annual Report of the CEPS Macroeconomic Policy Group, Daniel Gros, Juan F. Jimeno, Thomas Mayer, Niels Thygesen and Angel Ubide, July 2003

The Euro at 25, Special Report of the CEPS Macroeconomic Policy Group, Daniel Gros, Massimiliano Castelli, Juan Jimeno, Thomas Mayer and Niels Thygesen, December 2002

Fiscal and Monetary Policy for a Low-Speed Europe, 4th Annual Report of the CEPS Macroeconomic Policy Group, Daniel Gros, June 2002

Testing the Speed Limit for Europe, 3rd Macroeconomic Policy Group Report, Daniel Gros, Juan F. Jimeno, Carlo Monticelli, Guido Tabellini and Niels Thygesen, June 2001

Quo vadis euro? The Cost of Muddling Through, 2nd Report of the CEPS Macroeconomic Policy Group, Daniel Gros, Olivier Davanne, Michael Emerson, Thomas Mayer, Guido Tabellini and Niels Thygesen, May 2000

Macroeconomic Policy in the First Year of Euroland, 1st Annual Report of the CEPS Macroeconomic Policy Group, Daniel Gros, Olivier Blanchard, Michael Emerson, Thomas Mayer, Gilles Saint-Paul, Hans-Werner Sinn, Guido Tabellini, January 1999

Towards Economic and Monetary Union: Problems and Prospects, Daniel Gros for the CEPS Economic Policy Group, December 1995